Ecological Economics

Ecological Economics
A Political Economics Approach to Environment and Development

Peter Söderbaum

Earthscan Publications Ltd, London

First published in the UK in 2000 by
Earthscan Publications Ltd

A catalogue record for this book is available from the British Library

ISBN: 1 85383 685 0 paperback
      1 85383 686 9 hardback

Typesetting by PCS Mapping & DTP, Newcastle upon Tyne
Printed and bound by Creative Print and Design (Wales), Ebbw Vale
Cover design by Richard Reid

For a full list of publications please contact:

Earthscan Publications Ltd
120 Pentonville Road
London, N1 9JN, UK
Tel: +44 (0)171 278 0433
Fax: +44 (0)171 278 1142
Email: earthinfo@earthscan.co.uk
http://www.earthscan.co.uk

Earthscan is an editorially independent subsidiary of Kogan Page Ltd and publishes in
association with WWF-UK and the International Institute for Environment and
Development

This book is printed on elemental chlorine-free paper

Contents

List of Figures and Tables

FIGURES

TABLES

List of Acronyms and Abbreviations

ABB	Asea Brown Boveri
AFEE	Association for Evolutionary Economics
CBA	cost–benefit analysis
CeO	Citizen Environmental Organization
CRA	cost–revenue analysis
EAEPE	European Association for Evolutionary Political Economy
EDF	Environmental Defense Fund
EEC	European Economic Community (now EU)
EIA	environmental impact assessment
EIS	environmental impact statement
EMAS	Eco-Management and Audit Scheme (EU)
EMS	Environmental Management System
ESEE	European Society for Ecological Economics
EU	European Union
GATT	General Agreement on Tariffs and Trade
GDP	gross domestic product
IIA	integrated impact assessment
ISEE	International Society for Ecological Economics
ISO	International Standards Organization
LCA	life-cycle analysis
MIA	monetary impact assessment
NEPA	National Environmental Policy Act
NRDC	Natural Resources Defense Council
NUTEK	Swedish National Board for Industrial and Technical Development
PA	positional analysis
PEO	Political Economic Organization
PEP	Political Economic Person
ppm	parts per million
SIA	social impact assessment
UN	United Nations
WBCSD	World Business Council for Sustainable Development
WTO	World Trade Organization

Preface

Most people view science as part of the solution to a variety of problems. Here, I will argue that whilst science sometimes plays such a positive role, it can just as easily be part of the problems faced. In the present situation concerning environmental problems, it would seem wise to argue that no part or sector of society should be excluded from consideration in an attempt to identify problems and to seek improvements. Science and technology have played an important role in furthering a societal development path which is now, according to an increasing number of actors, regarded as far from satisfactory.

My arguments in this work tend mostly in the direction of the importance of pluralism, that is in favour of an open-minded attitude to various perspectives within a particular discipline or within science more generally. But such a pluralistic attitude does not imply that criticism of particular tendencies, perspectives or methods should be suppressed. One of the big mistakes in the evolution of science, as I see it, especially concerning a social science such as economics, is the dominance of a belief that science can exist in a vacuum, free from ideology. Such a 'value-free' or 'pure' science simply does not exist in relation to the issues of environment and development that will be discussed here, or that were the subject of the Rio de Janeiro Earth Summit talks and agreements in 1992. As argued by Gunnar Myrdal (1978), 'values are always with us' – in our work as scholars and in our endeavour to say something meaningful about how to tackle problems.

If we can come to an understanding of the role of values and ideology in relation to science, and particularly the social sciences, we may be more readily able to accept the differences in perspective and judgement of other scholars. It will also be easier to understand why some economists, myself included, are unhappy with the near-monopoly position in economics of the neo-classical view. The criticism is, of course, related to some extent to the logical structure of neo-classical economics. More important for many of us who prefer a pluralistic view, however, is the moral, ideological and political content of neo-classical economics. As I see it, a monopoly position for neo-classical economics at departments of economics means that the latter are reduced to organs of political propaganda. Or, to be more explicit; neo-classical economics can be seen as legitimizing a world view and development pattern that is now seen to engender many problems, for instance in relation to the environment. Of course, a statement of this kind itself represents a judgement on something that is exceedingly complex and which is in part a reflection of my own values.

The overall approach of this book can now, hopefully, be more easily understood. I shall systematically compare the neo-classical view, or rather some of its essential characteristics, with an alternative or complementary perspective that I believe will add to our ability to deal fruitfully with current issues. For example, neo-classical micro-economics includes a specific view of the human being referred to as Economic Man, and a specific view of organizations, as profit maximizing firms. Against this background one may suggest an alternative microeconomics based on individuals as responsible actors. What would a microeconomics look like which systematically considers how business operations affect Nature and the environment? Is there a microeconomics that takes environmental organizations seriously?

This attempt to put forward a proposal for a conceptual framework that differs from the neo-classical view in no way denies that the neo-classical view does have its uses nor that the views expressed in this book are the only viable alternatives. What should be remembered is that we already have a neo-classical environmental economics and that considerable investment in terms of money and effort has been made to improve this particular economics. The 'marginal utility' of dollars or pounds spent along neo-classical lines may therefore be small compared to what can be achieved for the same amount of money along alternative lines, for instance those associated with institutional or ecological economics. In my view, the traditions and more recent advances in other social sciences, such as sociology, political science, educational science, business management and so on, also have a great deal to offer to this development.

If one accepts that there is no value-free science in relation to environmental and development issues, then the next step is to try to clarify the values underlying a particular study. In the present case, ecological sustainability is a value of primary importance. This kind of sustainability cannot be achieved without considering the various social and monetary implications. With respect to the procedures we need to follow to achieve ecological sustainability, democracy is seen here as a meta-ideology and thus as an ideological platform that should be accepted by all. I believe quite simply that the values connected with democracy are of cardinal importance for any attempt to transform our present society.

A number of scholars at universities express concern on environmental issues. Some are mentioned below, while the contributions of others are reflected in the list of references. While acknowledging the importance of a dialogue among scholars, I would like to add, however, that many fruitful ideas come from actors outside the universities. Society as a whole appears to be involved in a co-operative learning process concerned with the problems it currently faces. Across society individuals learn about values, try to understand various processes and act to influence the outcomes of such processes. In this interactive process, scholars and students have a responsibility to contribute, but the same is true of other categories of actors such as politicians, administrators in public agencies, those engaged in environmental or religious organizations, those employed in business and financial institutions and so on. Moreover, partly because of inertia in the university system and a very strong epistemological tradition of beliefs in value neutrality, scientists will not always be the first to become aware of, understand and act upon new societal challenges.

This book is written for economists, both mainstream neo-classical economists and those who prefer to refer to themselves as institutionalists, socio-economists or ecological economists. However other academics or interested parties are just as important. Those with identities more connected with disciplines outside of economics should also be able to understand my arguments. In fact, while writing, I have also considered biologists and ecologists among my 'model readers'.

Acknowledgements

Some of the arguments presented here have appeared as articles in *Ecological Economics*, *The Journal of Economic Issues*, *The Journal of Interdisciplinary Economics*, as chapters in books and (in Swedish) in my previous book *Ekologisk ekonomi* (1993). While the argumentation is similar, the present text is new.

Among those who have encouraged me in my work and research efforts, I would like to mention Richard Norgaard, Herman Daly, Michael Common, Robert Goodland, Robert Costanza, Jonathan M Harris, Neva Goodwin, Ann-Mari Jansson, Carl Folke, all connected with the International Society for Ecological Economics. Sylvie Faucheux, Martin O'Connor, Clive Spash, Jan van der Straaten, Uno Simonis, Jörg Köhn, Juan Martinez-Alier, Irina Glazyrina, Paul Safonov and Beat Bürgenmeier, Silvio Funtowicz and Inge Röpke in the corresponding European Society are part of the same ecological economics project of co-operative learning. Mary E Clark and Eva Friman are two other persons engaged in the search for a different economics and social science. I derived great inspiration also from institutionalists such as Marc Tool and Paul Bush of the Association for Evolutionary Economics and a Finnish group of 'institutional environmental economists' at Helsinki University with Kauko Hahtola, Markku Turtiainen and Antti Leskinen.

While at the Swedish University of Agricultural Sciences in Uppsala, I enjoyed working with with Kjell-Åke Brorsson, Göran Forsberg, Gun Lidestav, Bengt Hillring and other members of an Ecological Economics research group as well as with students in ecological economics courses from 1992 to 1995. Among guest researchers at the Agricultural University, I would like to mention David Vail of Bowdoin College and Karel Pulkrab of the Czech University of Agriculture, Prague and at Mälardalen; Eva Cudlinova of the Institute of Landscape Ecology, Czech Academy of Sciences and Rajeswari S Raina of the National Institute of Science, Technology and Development Studies, New Delhi. Equally important are guest PhD students Lenka Kovarova (Czech University of Agriculture), Tatiana

Kluvankova (Institute of Forecasting SAS, Bratislava, Slovak Republic) and Stefan Brendstrup (Centre for Social Science Research on the Environment, CESAM, Aarhus University). Two PhD courses at Mälardalen University, Västerås and at Uppsala University, the Department of Business Studies have been important to me, with participants such as Sven Arrelöv, Robert Hjalmarsson, Patrik Holmström, Louise König, Glenn Sjöstrand, Ulrika Stavlöt, Fredrik Burström, Christer Westermark and Johan Sandström among others. I have also appreciated co-operating with Pekka Kuljunlahti and Hans Lundberg at the Department of Energy Technology, Anders Segerstedt and Theresa D'Errico at the Department of Business Studies as well as with Elvy Westlund, Hasse Odenö, P-O Rehnquist and Eva Björck-Åkesson at the university. In the field of 'business and environment', Gothenburg Research Institute with Rolf Wolff, Peter Dobers and others have provided an important source of inspiration and the same is true of the scientific programme committee of Stockholm Water Symposium with Malin Falkenmark, Lars Ulmgren, Ulf Ehlin, Klas Cederwall and Curt Forsberg.

The 200 students who are enrolled in the Ecological Economics undergraduate programme at Mälardalen University deserve a special mention. Some of them read the manuscript of this book in its early stages. Few things can be more important than the comments received from students.

The writing of this book was made possible through financial support from my previous employer, the Swedish University of Agricultural Sciences, Uppsala, and from Mälardalen University. Max Brandt, Uppsala, and Kim Allen at Earthscan have made a number of innovative proposals to improve my English. Last but not least, my thanks to my wife Eva and our children Hanna, Vilhelm, Jakob and Simon for their constant support.

Västerås, 29 June 1999
Peter Söderbaum

Chapter 1

Environmental and Other Problems

Before discussing the nature of environmental problems, it may be rewarding to consider just what we mean when we talk of a 'problem'. I suggest that perception of a problem refers to a perceived difference between an existing state of affairs and a desired one, relative to the particular actor, and taking into account his or her knowledge, experience, values and position in a social, institutional and physical context. In an alternative, more dynamic version of the definition of a problem, an actor negatively values the 'development path' and future outcomes of some ongoing activity, compared with the outcomes of an alternative development path.

This definition of 'problem' draws attention to the importance of values and ideology. Two different actors, A and B, may have different ideas about the present state of affairs and also what is desirable for the future. For example, A may argue that a lake that is undergoing a reduction in size due to eutrophication is a 'problem'. B on the other hand regards this change not as a problem but as a potential advantage. B might be a farmer who stands to gain by extending his acreage, albeit slowly, as a result of the eutrophication process.

The storage of nuclear waste can also illustrate the different ways of perceiving a phenomenon either as a problem – or not. A third actor, C, may trust and rely completely on the ability of scientists and engineers, the nuclear power companies and state civil servants to solve this problem. C may not even accept that nuclear waste is or poses a problem at all. A fourth actor, D, on the other hand, is of the opinion that it is highly likely that the problem of disposing of nuclear waste can never be satisfactorily solved. D may lay great weight on a precautionary principle – that nuclear waste should never have been produced in the first place; but, in view of its existence, that nuclear reactors should be closed down as soon as possible to prevent the production of even more waste.

Clearly actors C and D differ in their views about the importance or seriousness of problems in society. C may perceive business expansion and profitability at the micro-level and 'economic growth' measured in terms of GDP at the national level as lying at the heart of her or his value orientation, whereas impacts on ecosystems and depletion of natural resources are secondary or even minor matters. C may regard any deterioration of the competitiveness of his or her country's industrial base as a serious problem. Implicit in such an ideological orientation is the belief that by constantly increasing GDP one can solve virtually all the problems that the country may face – environmental problems included.

Actor D, characterized here as 'green' in valuational or ideological orientation, questions the idea of GDP growth as the all-important measure of progress in society. D believes that in the present circumstances, continuing GDP growth can lead to more rather than fewer problems and he or she emphasizes that new visions and ideologies for societal development are important. Ideas about ecological sustainability need to be formulated and a choice of ways to move in that direction need to be identified.

When we now contrast the outlook of C with that of D, it is clear that the two actors have different ideas concerning the problems or issues confronting society. C gives economic growth and international competitiveness top priority on his or her 'personal agenda'. D on the other hand favours ecological sustainability and wise husbandry of natural resources. A whole plethora of problems are of importance both for society as a whole and for the individual. In a sense, all these issues compete for our attention. Each individual actor may, in principle, have his or her own agenda or list of priorities for such problems. Within society there will also be predominant agendas of particular collectives such as firms or other organizations, local communities, nations, or a group of nations such as the European Union. It is even possible to speak of an agenda on a global level, as reflected for instance in international agreements or in the policies and activities of institutions such as the UN or the World Bank.

THE IMPORTANCE OF IDEOLOGY

When acting in a specific role, each individual uses her or his own world view or ideology as a basis for their own agenda or list of priorities. As we have seen, the agenda of any organization similarly reflects its own dominant values. Ideology is used here in a broad sense and refers to 'ideas about means–ends relationships' in any sphere of human activity. In textbooks on political ideologies (Eccleshall et al, 1994), only established ideas about means–ends relationships, such as liberalism, social-ism, conservatism and various newer -isms like 'ecologism' and 'feminism' qualify as 'ideologies'. Ideas about means and ends lying closer to operational activities in organizations, or nearer to private life, will be included here among ideologies. For example, one may contrast various 'health care ideologies'; for instance those emphasizing central-ized systems, versus others suggesting that decentralization offers many advantages. Similarly, there are different 'environmental ideologies', some founded on technological optimism, others on the aforemen-tioned 'principle of cautiousness'. Even in the context of a school classroom or private household, our actions are formed by our beliefs concerning fruitful means–ends relationships. We need ideas, images or models to guide us through the complexities of the real world.

Most economists have been reluctant to refer to ideologies and world views, but Douglas North is an exception. In a footnote in his book *Institutions, Institutional Change and Economic Performance*, he makes the following statement:

> *By ideology, I mean the subjective perceptions (models, theories) all people possess to explain the world around them. Whether at the microlevel of individual relationships or at the macrolevel of organized ideologies providing integrated explanations of the past and the present, such as commu-nism or religions, the* theories *individuals construct are* colored *by normative views of how the world should be organized* (North, 1990, p23, original emphasis).

Ideologies in the present sense are based on beliefs. Such beliefs consist not only of factual elements, but also of expectations about the possible outcomes of acting according to one particular ideology rather than another. An ideology may be more or less established on the societal level and similarly more or less adopted by an individual. It may be more or less well formulated or logically coherent. Even if it is perceived by the individual as shaky or fragmentary an ideology may nevertheless serve as a guide to action. The term I shall use for the fragmentary and uncertain nature of the images and ideas that guide us is 'ideological orientation'.

SCIENCE AND IDEOLOGY

We assume here that each individual is guided by an 'ideological orien-tation' and that ideas and images are important elements of any such orientation. But where do these ideas and images come from? One answer is that many of the ideas that play a role in our daily life have their origin in, or are legitimized by, science. According to John Maynard Keynes, economists and political philosophers in particular have contributed greatly in this regard:

> *The ideas of economists and political philosophers, both when they are right and when they are wrong, are more powerful than is commonly understood. Indeed the world is ruled by little else. Practical men, who believe themselves to be quite exempt from any intellectual influences, are usually the slaves of some defunct economist* (from Fusfeld, 1994, p1).

Interpreting the 'market' mechanistically in terms of 'supply' and 'demand' with associated beliefs in 'the invisible hand' – a concept used by Adam Smith but older in origin – is an example of the sort of idea that features in current public debate and in the decision-making and daily activities of politicians, civil servants and businessmen. Other ideas that have become common are the views of organizations as 'profit maximizing firms' and of human beings as 'consumers' who maximize utility.

Keynes' statement is worth considering, but should be qualified in certain respects. There is today quite a choice in terms of 'defunct economists'. Even a particular economist, take Adam Smith for instance, can be interpreted in more than one way. I share Keynes' judgement that 'practical men' are dependent on the ideas of economists, but would like to emphasize that not only dead economists but also living ones are responsible for this state of affairs. If there is a slavery relationship, as suggested by Keynes, the masters are not necessarily far away in terms of time and space. In terms of the supply of economic ideas, present-day neo-classicists have established a near-monopoly position at departments of economics and this is, in my opinion, a major danger confronting modern society. Dictatorship in the sphere of economic ideas is as bad as in any other field of public life.

One reason why such a form of monopoly is problematical has to do with our interpretation of the role of science in society. Keynes himself, in the above quotation, speaks of ideas as if they are either true or false or, to use his words, 'right' or 'wrong'. Accordingly, economists – and perhaps also the 'political philosophers' referred to by Keynes – seek truth, and when they believe themselves to have succeeded in this endeavour, disseminate their knowledge to various actors in society and to the general public.

Personally, I do not believe that the interaction between scientists and other actors in society (or 'practical men') is well described as one of a uni-directional distribution of knowledge. Ideas flow in both directions and the power of 'practical men' in influencing social science should not be underestimated. The latter may, for instance, choose to 'accept' certain ideas coming from science while disregarding other contributions. By generating their own ideas and selectively supporting parts of the scientific community, they can be active participants in a dialogue about specific issues and the future of society more generally.

I will therefore emphasize here a second model, referred to as an actor-network model or, alternatively, an interaction model. As part of this view, models, theories and conceptual frameworks – especially in the social sciences – should not be regarded as exclusively scientific matters, but also as ideological concerns. Concepts and theories are, at least in part, socially constructed to serve specific scientific and ideological purposes. Acceptance of specific conceptual simplifications (and even more complex conceptual frameworks) such as the aforementioned 'invisible hand', is as much a matter of ideology as of science. In other words, there is no pure or value-free science.

When we work with the interaction model, we begin to recognize that university scholars as well as 'practical men', such as business leaders, are guided by their 'ideological orientations' and may well have ideas that they want to implant in other actors. Economists and political philosophers have power, but conversely those engaged in practical affairs can also exercise influence on actors in the universities. One may ask, for example, why a particular view of organizations (such as profit maximizing firms) becomes accepted and popular among practical men while other competing ideas find fewer supporters. An initial answer, and more in line with Keynes' argument above, is that the actors at the universities teach economics in a monistic fashion and in this way promote certain ideas. But in addition, there is a 'demand' side (in the 'market' of ideas) with actors, both individually and as organizations, exercising a preference and accepting only specific views of organizations (as 'firms' in the neo-classical sense). In this way the actors' often entrenched thought patterns and value orientations are legitimized by 'science'. A focus on the financial and monetary aspects of organizational practice may facilitate life for business actors, at least in the short run, when compared with an alternative view of the organization where non-monetary (eg social, environmental) impacts are systematically made visible in accounting systems, publicity, etc. With a focus on profit maximizing, that is a kind of 'monetary reductionism', issues such as the social responsibility of business can effectively be played down.

While there are actors who are happy with the current state of affairs in departments of economics, other actors may hold ideologies that depart significantly from those built into neo-classical economics. They may 'demand' ideas which are not 'supplied' as part of mainstream economics. They may believe in and rely on their own mental faculties or have listened to sources other than neo-classical economists. They may be concerned about ecosystems, about natural resources, and feel that they bear a degree of social responsibility in relation to various affected sections of society. Rather than neglecting such 'demands' for an alternative conceptual framework and theory, university scholars should be sensitive to criticism of mainstream approaches and be ready to reconsider their conceptual framework and theory.

Interaction and dialogue within the scientific community with all its different disciplines, within the community of 'practical men' as well as between scholars and practical men will mean that new ideas – wherever they come from – will be tested. Competition in the world of ideas will replace monopoly. I believe that regarding interaction in society as a process of mutual learning, where science as well as ideology is involved, gives a better representation of reality than does the traditional 'truth dissemination model'. But according to the very logic of our second model, which sees science and ideology as interconnected, it also serves my own ideological purpose in the search for an economics that will help us to deal with environmental problems in a fruitful manner.

While not excluding the possibility of neo-classical economists changing their position, I see the best hope of change coming mainly from two other sources. As hinted at by Keynes in the quotation above, other humanistic and social sciences exist in addition to economics. These disciplines also supply ideas that various actors consider relevant. Philosophers such as Mark Sagoff may criticize ideas put forward by economists (Sagoff, 1988); Amitai Etzioni and other sociologists may take an interest in economics and suggest alternatives to 'economic man' assumptions (Etzioni, 1988, 1992); political scientists may take part in the dialogue on the basis of an interdisciplinary approach referred to as 'policy science' (Fischer, 1990), to mention just a few examples.

In addition to the humanistic and social sciences, there are actors within business, environmental, religious and other organizations who have a lot to offer the dialogue on the environment and development. As a scholar, I may learn just as much from my interaction with politicians, business leaders, environmentalists and ordinary citizens as from my colleagues. If non-neo-classical schools of thought are to be strengthened or there is to be a 'new' economics, the initiative and driving force will not come exclusively from scholars at departments of economics. Also those who 'demand' conceptual frameworks, or paradigms with specific characteristics, will play an important role.

Neo-Classical Economics

How do neo-classical economists approach environmental problems? To respond to this question, it would seem appropriate to say a few words on the history of economic ideas. As the term suggests, neo-classical economics is regarded as a new version of economics when compared with the classical version. Of the classical economists, Adam Smith is perhaps the best known with his celebrated book *An Inquiry into the Nature and Causes of the Wealth of Nations*, published in 1776. David Ricardo and Thomas Malthus are two other influential and well-known classical economists.

Adam Smith's ideas about 'division of labour' and the self-adjusting market or the 'invisible hand', that produces the best possible outcome for society as a whole, are still influential in public debate and the same can be said of David Ricardo's principles of international trade. At the time when Smith wrote his book and until the advent of neo-classical economics a century later, the discipline was referred to as 'political economy' or 'political economics'. Ricardo's book *Principles of Political Economy and Taxation* from 1817 is a good example.

The era of neo-classical economics started around the 1870s and is associated with the writings of Karl Menger, William Stanley Jevons and Leon Walras among others. While building on many of the classical economists' ideas about markets and international trade, they tried to refine the theory and to express it in mathematical terms. Value was connected with an individual's utility of a commodity in use and not exclusively, as in classical theory, with the labour input necessary to produce that commodity. As part of the new approach to economics, a principle of diminishing marginal utility was formulated, which stated that a consumer who, for instance, considers how many slices of bread she or he will consume per day, is expected to enjoy the first slices of bread more than the ones that follow. At some stage the utility added by consuming an additional slice decreases.

The concept of market equilibrium was introduced and elaborated by Alfred Marshall in the late 19th century. Thinking in terms of a balance or 'equilibrium' between the supply of and demand for a commodity became an important part of neo-classical theory. It is on ideas of this kind that present-day neo-classical economics is built. In endeavouring to characterize neo-classical economics, I would suggest the following features:

1   The market lies at the heart of the analysis and is perceived in terms of the supply and demand of homogeneous commodities (goods and services). All market actors possess complete information about alternatives of choice and their impacts. Balance or equilibrium between supply and demand is emphasized. There is an emphasis on 'static analysis', that is analysis that refers to a point in time. Changes in demand and/or supply as well as the manipulation of markets by governments are portrayed as a shift from one equilibrium point to another. This is referred to as 'comparative static analysis'. Other historical or dynamic aspects are played down.
2   Welfare is seen to be connected to the utility of individuals who buy commodities on the market within the scope of their monetary budget and then 'consume' those commodities. A larger monetary income implies increased welfare, since more commodities can be consumed.
3   The kinds of organization taken seriously in the analysis are referred to as 'firms'. Firms supply commodities and maximize their profits by considering monetary costs and revenues. Analysis in terms of the marginal (monetary) costs and revenues of producing one extra unit of a commodity is important when establishing the level of production that maximizes profits.
4   The national economy is seen as consisting essentially of firms and households. Firms produce and sell commodities to households. For their production, firms also buy labour from the households and raw material from other firms. Households supply labour to get a pecuniary income with which to purchase commodities. This simple model can be extended to include the national government which collects taxes and may procure commodities directly on the market or transfer money from one section of the population to another. International trade and international flows of labour and money capital are other possible extensions of the original model. (It should be noted that this is essentially a model where money and commodities are transferred between firms and households and where labour and capital may also move in response to market forces.)

The neo-classical paradigm is furthermore founded on certain epistemological (theory of science) ideas:

5   One such idea is monism, meaning that the neo-classical paradigm tends to exclude other theoretical perspectives in economics. Other social science perspectives also tend to be excluded. Neo-classical economists realize that there are tensions within their theoretical perspective or paradigm. These tensions may lead to a further sharpening of the paradigm in a process of knowledge accumulation. To the extent that neo-classical economists realize that their paradigm may, at some time in the future, fail to explain contemporary phenomena or solve our current problems, they will probably think in terms of a paradigm-shift (Kuhn, 1970). This means that some new paradigm must replace the neo-classical one. In this respect, most neo-classicists are still far from the pluralism and 'paradigm coexistence' advocated in this work.

6   Neo-classical economists tend to regard physics and other natural sciences as their ideal. Reasoning in terms of equilibrium between the 'forces' of supply and demand is part of this view. The scholar is seen as standing apart and objectively observing what is taking place in the economy. He or she is looking for regularities of a mechanistic kind, very similar to the natural laws of physics. 'Objectivity' and 'value neutrality' are related ideas, originating largely from physics or from more general ideas about the 'good science' of the 19th century. Whereas classical economists openly declared the political element of their discipline, the neo-classicists hoped to 'purify' economics from political elements. 'Political economics' became 'economics' and neo-classical economists are, even today, reluctant to admit the political element of their theories and methods.

ENVIRONMENTAL PROBLEMS AND NEO-CLASSICAL ECONOMICS

An increased understanding of the urgency of tackling environmental problems has led to a relatively new branch of neo-classical economics – referred to as 'environmental economics'. It represents an extension of neo-classical economics and is easier to understand if one knows something about the paradigm as a whole and its historical development.

It has already been observed that neo-classical economics focuses on markets. Neo-classical environmental economics is no exception, as is evident in the more popular textbooks (Pearce et al, 1989; Pearce and Turner, 1990; Tietenberg, 1992). While the market is generally expected to perform well, especially under circumstances of competition between firms, it may occasionally fail. The existence of environmental problems is connected with such 'market failures'. To exemplify this, we can think of a firm, A, producing and selling motor lawnmowers. B buys one to use in his or her garden. As everyone knows, using these machines is connected with pollution and noise. B may be affected while using the mower, and neighbours, C and D, may also suffer. Negative impacts on C and D are referred to as being 'external' or as 'externalities' and environmental problems are connected with such 'third party' impacts.

The terminology is of interest here. The factors which are 'internal' and 'external' are defined in relation to specific market transactions, such as the one between A and B. It is assumed that A and B know what they are doing and that the prices and other conditions of market exchange are acceptable to both trading parties. But some parties, external to the market transaction may suffer and when this is the case, neo-classicists speak of negative externalities. To 'solve' environmental problems, neo-classical economists therefore usually make the recommendation that externalities should be 'internalized'. In our example this would entail putting a 'correct' price on the externalities by placing an environmental charge on the power lawnmower sold and/or on the fuel used for such machines. Market actors should pay the total cost or 'full price', that is one which includes a consideration of negative externalities. In this way, negative externalities will be reduced somewhat, although not eliminated, the idea being that there is some 'optimal level of pollution control'.

Today, so-called externalities are taken seriously by most neo-classical environmental economists, but there was a time when such impacts were regarded as secondary, unintended impacts, unavoidable side effects, and so on. From one of my first lectures in environmental economics in the early 1970s, I remember a biology student who questioned my vocabulary when speaking about externalities in relation to market transactions. He argued that since it had been announced that the course was on environmental management, then environmental impacts, rather than the market transaction, should be the main subject: 'Environmental impacts should be regarded as "internal", while those market impacts could be considered as less important and "external".'

It should be noted that in the neo-classical view, it is the market as a mechanistic phenomenon which fails rather than the market actors themselves. Such criticism of individuals as actors for the way that they maximize utility (sometimes using environmentally detrimental products) or profit seems to be taboo as part of the neo-classical position. The national government may be held responsible to some extent, however, and is expected to correct the functioning of the market by imposing environmental charges or taxes. While everyone realizes that there are innumerable negative externalities, few governments have as yet introduced many environmental charges. Why is this so? One reason might be that environmental economists and many political actors are so fond of 'the market' that they have difficulty in conceding that it can fail. Another possible reason is that full recognition of all externalities might take us several steps away from a market economy in the direction of a planned economy, where almost every price is settled by state agencies in an attempt to reflect prevailing externalities.

According to the neo-classical view, governments may also fail by transferring tax revenues to activities which are detrimental to the environment. An often-used example from Sweden concerns the government subsidising the construction of tracks for logging operations in high mountains close to the tree limit. Such subsidies make it profitable for timber companies to exploit old forests, which are known to contain rare species and therefore, according to many, should be conserved for the future.

From the above reasoning, it should be clear that something *could* be achieved through neo-classical analysis. To improve environmental performance the government can manipulate prices and subsidies. (When neo-classical economists claim to be able to identify 'correct' prices or environmental charges from the point of view of societal resource allocation, there is more reason for scepticism, a point to which we will return later.)

But the special scope of neo-classical analysis should also be noted. From a more critical stance, it can be argued that neo-classicists tend to conceptualize environmental problems to fit the neo-classical paradigm. Since the basic features of neo-classical theory are unchanged, one might get the impression that the important task facing economists is to save the neo-classical paradigm, rather than respond to environmental threats. Or, to use another terminology, protecting the conceptual framework of neo-classical economics seems to be far more important than protecting the environment or nature.

Neo-classical economists regard as innovative and exciting the idea of interpreting environmental problems in terms of markets and prices. But actors not indoctrinated in this particular paradigm may perceive the same idea as strange. Ecosystem services and other phenomena related to the environment or natural resources are simply interpreted as other categories of commodities. Like conventional commodities, environmental ones can be bought and sold in actual or imagined markets. This means that the environment becomes 'tradable' in the sense that natural resources and various forms of life can be replaced by other resources. Money is referred to as a 'common denominator' and environmental impacts, like other impacts, are valued in monetary terms. Sometimes reference is made to actual markets to get information about such values. In other cases, questionnaires are used to ascertain consumers' values in terms of their 'willingness to pay' for specific environmental commodities sold in 'hypothetical' or imagined markets. (More rarely, values refer to 'willingness to accept' environmental damage.) Cost–benefit analysis, CBA, is used in monetary terms to arrive at 'solutions' that are said to be 'optimal' from a societal point of view.

The value of the CBA method itself depends on a consensus in society about the specific ethics or ideology of CBA. Similarly, there has to be a consensus about how to value negative environmental impacts as part of the attempt to find an optimal level of pollution control through marginal analysis. If no such consensus exists, the aforementioned neo-classical approaches are no longer more relevant and useful than other valuational rules capable of indicating 'solutions' to problems (cf Mishan, 1980; Söderbaum, 1983). It is suggested here that the best one can do in a democratic society with multifarious opinions and ideologies (rather than one) is to try to elucidate an issue for actors and interested parties (who will differ among themselves with respect to position, values and ideology), rather than to try to 'solve' it.

FACING COMPLEXITY

Without excluding the possible value of simplistic models, it will be suggested here that one should try to face complexity rather than assume it away. If reality is complex, then we have to live with this complexity, or at least a considerable part of it.

> *We live in a world that is becoming increasingly complex.*
> *Unfortunately our styles of thinking rarely match this*
> *complexity. We often end up persuading ourselves that*
> *everything is more simple than it actually is, dealing with*
> *complexity by presuming that it does not really exist*
> (Morgan, 1986, p16).

The evolution of science at the universities has been characterized by specialization and compartmentalization. Connected with this development is the strengthening of a belief that not only scientific problems (in some limited sense) but also societal problems can be solved within the scope of a single discipline. What is now becoming increasingly understood is that most societal problems – and environmental problems belong to this category – are multifactorial and multidimensional in character. They require a transdisciplinary approach rather than a single discipline approach.

One aspect of this recognition that environmental problems cross different disciplines, is an understanding that problems do not reside exclusively 'out there in the fields'. While the measurement of environmental parameters – such as the pH-value of a lake at a particular place at succeeding points in time – is important, it is at the same time increasingly understood that there is a human side to the problems encountered. Individuals, their organizations and society at large, influence what goes on in the lake, and in the environment more generally, and human beings are led by their world views, ideologies and ethical considerations. This means that world view, ideology, ethics and related scientific perspectives all have to be included in any attempt to reduce degradation of the environment or to improve the state of the environment.

TOULMIN ON THE EVOLUTION OF WORLD VIEWS

The dominant world view in our societies is often referred to as 'modernism' (Toulmin, 1990; Norgaard, 1994). Modernism, as understood here, is based on a strong belief in science and on specific ideas of rationality in the organization of society. According to Stephen Toulmin, the 'modern' world view, which is largely associated with names such as René Descartes and later Isaac Newton, entailed a move away from humanism. More precisely, it was a movement:

- from the oral to the written;
- from the particular to the universal;
- from the local to the general; and
- from the timely to the timeless.

In terms of philosophy, this 'modernism' represented a change in emphasis from practical philosophy to a theoretical philosophy that used the abstract language of mathematics. From 1970 onwards, this path has, again according to Toulmin, been regarded as a failure by a significant number of respected philosophers such as Richard Rorty and Martin Heidegger. Their criticism in turn has paved the way for a return to practical philosophy, a change that involved an increased interest in 'the oral', that is in rhetoric, or in present-day language, in public dialogue. Ideas about an ethics formulated in universal terms is played down in favour of a situational 'case ethics', reflecting the particular circumstances of a given situation. The study of individual cases became more respected, as opposed to logical reasoning, with the purpose of finding general laws. History and 'timeboundedness' became important as opposed to an exclusive reliance on laws formulated in a timeless manner. In more general terms, context became relevant and the previous tendency to decontextualize with respect to person, time, place, and so on was replaced by an effort to 'recontextualize'. Stephen Toulmin sees this as a return to humanism and renaissance. Contextualism at the same time represents an attack on beliefs in a unified science. A more humble attitude is warranted for scientists, who should learn to live with some degree of uncertainty and ambiguity.

Toulmin does not say much about the development in economics. But as I see it, neo-classical economics fits well into the previously drawn picture of modernism. The emphasis on pure theory and mathematics makes one think in terms of a parallel with theoretical philosophy. Neo-classical economics aims at general timeless (equilibrium) laws and is in many ways a decontextualized theory. History is unimportant. Uncertainty and ambiguity is not an issue in a theory that assumes perfect information. Other schools of thought in economics, such as institutionalism, and other social sciences, such as business management, have followed a different evolutionary path, as we will see. This is exemplified by case studies, which have long been a respected way of acquiring knowledge in business management research.

MANY KINDS OF FAILURE OR SUCCESS

In summarizing, one may therefore argue that the neo-classical attempt to explain specific environmental problems as representing either 'market failure' or 'government failure' should be understood on the basis of the peculiarities of the neo-classical paradigm. A different and broader frame of reference will make us see a different set of potential failures.

As part of such a more complex view of environmental and societal issues, we have to include at least the following *potential* and interrelated failures:

* failure of world view;
* failure of ideology;
* failure of science in general and of specific paradigms;

- institutional failure (where the failures of markets and government, according to neo-classical theory, represent special cases);
- failure of individuals in specific roles and in their overall life-styles;
- failure of organizations of various kinds (business corporations, universities, environmental organizations, churches etc).

This list of possible failures can no doubt be extended or rephrased, but it allows for a broader analysis and dialogue than is the case with the neo-classical view. Neo-classical economists do not discuss the relationships between their paradigm and the predominant or other world views or ideologies of a particular society. Along Toulmin's lines of reasoning, one may ask if there is any interest at all in particular societies, the emphasis instead being on a globally valid model society in market terms. The project is one which most intellectuals would consider impossible; claiming value neutrality while at the same time designing a model society and supplying rules for 'correct' valuation of particular courses of action within the scope of that society.

I will not repeat here the mistake of neo-classicists by arguing that I know the 'correct' world view, ideology or institutional structure for a model society. I certainly have preferences, which are visible in the present book, and which point in certain directions, but my main argument is one of pluralism. Let us broaden our horizons and debate different world views, ideologies, theories of science and paradigms both within particular disciplines and on a transdisciplinary level.

Although the 'modern' world view may have succeeded in some important respects, it has failed in others. Science has been successful in certain areas and on certain terms, but ideas about value neutrality and objectivity may also have contributed to irresponsibility among scholars. As suggested by Keynes in the earlier quotation, economics has played a particular role in formulating our world views and also our ideologies. Today, a liberal market ideology, which is sometimes referred to as 'economism' (but for which I would prefer the clarifying term 'neo-classical economism'), appears to be dominating political discourse in many parts of the world.

Neo-classicism as an ideology can be exemplified by the reductionist tendencies to connect welfare with GDP per capita and with the view of individuals as maximizing utility or of organizations as firms maximizing monetary profits. Other views are thereby automatically played down or excluded.

Related to values and ideology are the institutional arrangements, that is the issues of law, organization, power relationships and conflicts of interest. In relation to this set of factors, there is a possibility of failure, where 'government failure' in the sense of the neo-classical paradigm, suggests adjustments that can be described as marginal or minor. One case in point where major institutional changes are taken seriously is David Korten's book *When Corporations Rule the World* (1995). According to Korten, citizens in all democracies are losing power and influence to transnational corporations with limited responsibilities. We shall return to this argument later in this volume. So, while acknowledging that minor changes in the right direction are of importance, we should not exclude the possibility of more fundamental institutional reforms. In contemplating such possibilities, some degree of pluralism seems to be a good idea.

Individuals and organizations may 'fail' in relation to a specific definition of ecological sustainability. They may thereby aggravate environmental and social problems. Individuals may fail as market actors, as parents, as citizens and even as professionals. Organizations may similarly fail by not acting, or acting in the wrong way, when judged from the point of view of ecological sustainability. It seems important to discuss critically the roles and responsibilities of business corporations, environmental organizations, universities and even religious groups in relation to environmental issues. Early environmentalists met considerable hostility from business representatives. This may be true even today, but in my experience a new tendency is for business actors to seek critical examination and help in the form of constructive proposals. They may themselves criticize the universities, where scholars too often behave opportunistically in relation to a power situation that may be misconceived or may no longer exist. It is possible that actors outside universities increasingly perceive a majority of scholars as sleeping behind curtains of objectivity and imagined value neutrality.

While an open attitude to various possible kinds of failure seems warranted, the same open-mindedness will help us see a number of positive examples as well. World views that represent alternatives to the above-mentioned 'modernism' are gaining increasing support in science as well as in other parts of society. Among ideologies, 'ecologism' is, as we will see, an alternative to market liberalization and globalization. Social sciences other than economics are gaining ground in the dialogue concerning environmental issues and even within economics there are competitors to the neo-classical outlook.

Public environmental awareness is growing and this is reflected in behaviour and in changing roles and life-styles. An increasing number of actors within governmental agencies, universities, business corporations, environmental and religious organizations, and so on are working assiduously in response to environmental threats and the positive option of building a sustainable society. Certification schemes such as ISO 14000 and the European Union's EMAS (Eco-Management and

Audit Scheme) are playing an increasing role in business. Regulation in the form of environmental charges imposed or subsidies awarded by national governments will always have a role, but will never be enough. Initiatives at a local level and networks within local municipalities and regions can be equally important. The Rio de Janeiro agreements from 1992 and its Agenda 21 legitimate such initiatives and change processes.

It is open to conjecture whether the negative or positive examples will gain the ascendancy. If the present trends continue, there would appear to be good reason for some degree of optimism. My chief purpose with this book, however, is not to stand outside, objectively observing what happens to the environment, but rather to get involved and to try to make things happen in a step-by-step, progressive fashion.

Chapter 2

Ecological Economics

If awareness of environmental problems has increased in society generally, this must also be true of a number of specific actor categories.
Scholars and students at universities are hopefully not an exception to
this trend. Although, as argued earlier, scientists are not necessarily
the first to change their way of thinking, their ideologies and behaviour, it seems reasonable to suggest that the numbers of scientists and
students concerned about environmental problems are increasing in
most countries. One way of showing concern openly in the scientific
community is to start an organization for scholarly co-operation.
Environmental concerns have not only influenced the evolutionary
patterns of scientific organizations, but have also been influential in
the establishment of new associations. I will now highlight some of the
events behind the emergence of one such organization, the
International Society for Ecological Economics.

When we consider the founding of an association, we will find
different stories being told by the different actors who were involved.
My attempt is therefore just one of many possible versions. Hopefully,
some of the facts will be judged relevant for many observers and
participants, facts that will limit the freedom of the serious 'story-
teller'. Nevertheless, the story is valid and legitimate for me as a
person and, as we will see later in this chapter, personality is one of
the factors that have to be discussed as part of epistemology.

In 1982, a so-called Wallenberg symposium was arranged in
Stockholm. Two scholars, Ann-Mari Jansson, an ecologist, and her
husband, Bengt-Owe Jansson, a marine biologist, were of the opinion
that a dialogue between ecologists and economists might be worth-
while. At that time, neo-classical economics had been extended to
cover environmental issues and the main arguments about the
'polluter-pays principle' and cost–benefit analysis had been developed.
The idea of the Janssons, as I understand it, was to invite an equal
number of well-known environmental economists and well-known

ecologists to present their views about environmental issues and to listen to each other. Economists might learn from ecologists and vice versa and some new ideas might emerge from the whole experiment. The papers presented at the symposium were published and gave a good picture of the state of the art at the time (Jansson, 1984).

A similar symposium was organized by Juan Martinez-Alier in Barcelona, Spain, in 1987. In 1989, the first issue of the *Ecological Economics* journal appeared and in 1990 the International Society for Ecological Economics (ISEE) was founded. Its first international conference, with about 350 participants, was arranged on the premises of the World Bank, Washington, DC. Similar international conferences have since been held in Stockholm (1992), San José, Costa Rica (1994), Boston (1996) and Santiago, Chile (1998). Regional groups, affiliated to the international association have been established in, for example, Russia, Australia/New Zealand and Europe. The latter organization, European Society for Ecological Economics (ESEE), held its first meeting in Paris in May 1996 and its second meeting in Geneva in 1998, each with more than 300 participants.

Many young researchers have joined these associations and one may only speculate about their motives. In the field of environmental problems, single discipline approaches are limited, while transdisciplinary approaches offer many advantages. Moreover, the commitment to take environmental problems seriously (rather than standing outside observing developments in an allegedly value-neutral way) could be attractive to young scholars.

WHAT IS ECOLOGICAL ECONOMICS?

Ecological economics can be described as a transdisciplinary field of study rather than a single discipline. Scholars from economics and ecology can contribute, but so too can those who have their main background in other disciplines. Social sciences other than economics – such as sociology, political science, business management, educational science – have a role to play and the same can be said of the humanities, as well as of the natural and engineering sciences.

What matters is whether there is a concern for the environmental problems of contemporary society. A second characteristic of ecological economics is therefore a commitment or mission to engage in public debate and practical action with a view to dealing constructively with the problems. Ecological sustainability is the vision (although there are different interpretations of this term) and the idea is to develop theories and means that will bring us closer to the ideal of a sustainable society.

For most students who refer to themselves as ecological economists, there is also an element of humility, not only in relation to the
challenges confronting us, but also in relation to science and our own
research activities. We feel that over the years, science has actually
aggravated problems and not just contributed by supplying 'solutions'.
For this and other reasons, a pluralistic attitude is recommended. In
the first issue of *Ecological Economics*, the editor maintained that 'a
large measure of conceptual pluralism' is warranted. There is probably
no single 'right approach' or paradigm. This point was further elaborated as follows:

> *Environmental and resource economics, as it is currently
> practiced, covers only the application of neo-classical
> economics to environmental and resource problems. Ecology,
> as it is currently practiced, sometimes deals with human
> impacts on ecosystems, but the more common tendency is to
> stick to 'natural' systems.* Ecological Economics *aims to
> extend these modest areas of overlap. It will include neo-
> classical environmental economics and ecological impact
> studies as subsets, but will also encourage new ways of
> thinking about the linkages between ecological and
> economic systems* (Costanza, 1989, p1).

It should be made clear, however, that pluralism does not mean that
'anything goes'. Each scholar may have strong preferences in terms of
theoretical perspectives and methods. Pluralism in our sense therefore
means that such preferences are combined with a willingness to listen
and learn. This open-minded attitude implies that even a neo-classical
environmental economist can refer to her- or himself as an ecological
economist, if she or he so prefers. Connected to the Academy of
Sciences in Stockholm is the Beijer International Institute of Ecological
Economics, which since its inception has had a neo-classical environmental economist as its director and a majority of similarly inclined
economists on the board. The preferences of the present author tend
to be in the direction of institutional economics and the argument of
this book can be described as 'an institutional version of ecological
economics'. The meaning of institutional economics will be discussed
later on in this chapter.

Since ecological economics is an open field in the above sense, one
can only speculate about the sympathies of those who have chosen to
join ISEE or ESEE rather than the older organizations for neo-classical
environmental economists. Here, I make the judgement that most
ecological economists, albeit with varying motives, are sceptical of

pretensions about the sufficiency of the neo-classical perspective. Most of us seek and present alternative theoretical perspectives and tools. This holds true for members of ISEE, but perhaps even more so for ESEE. In the first newsletter from ESEE, one of the prominent members of the association, René Passet, argues as follows:

> *The very name of the Society indicates the double nature of the needs that it will have to answer to. First, and in opposition to the 'conventional wisdom', ESEE must insist on the originality of an* ecological economic *science. The encounter of economics with the biosphere cannot be limited to the unveiling of new fields of application while economics remains unchanged in essence. Ecological economists must show that, far beyond a simple internalisation of externalities or contingent valuations, the task is to rethink the economic science itself, by means of a trans-disciplinary approach. This, as indicated by the 'trans-' prefix ('across' and 'beyond'), goes across disciplines, brings them together, and goes beyond them, in a conception of the human being that leads to the ethical question of the double human responsibility: the intragenerational and the intergenerational responsibilities* (Passet, 1997, p2).

I support this judgement with respect to directions in which to search; a readiness to look for alternatives to the neo-classical perspective, an emphasis on transdisciplinary approaches and on the need to articulate ethical issues as part of economics. Among the books published in Ecological Economics and which give a good overview of the subject, I would like to mention two, one edited by Costanza (1991) and the other by Krishnan et al (1995). A number of collections of papers presented at conferences have been produced (Faucheux et al, 1998, O'Connor and Spash, 1999, Köhn et al, 1999), and from the textbooks available I would like to mention one by Robert Costanza, John Cumberland, Herman Daly, Robert Goodland and Richard Norgaard (1997).

INSTITUTIONAL ECONOMICS

When a group of economists in the 1870s launched their 'pure' or 'value-free' mathematical economics, there were other economists who were less enthusiastic about this new development. At least two other lines of thought can be traced back to the classical economists (see for instance Fusfeld 1994). One can be described as 'socialist', but the one that interests us more is referred to as 'institutionalist'. So-called utopian socialists like Robert Owen in Britain and Charles Fourier in France who were active in the early 19th century represent the first tradition. They were followed by Karl Marx who wrote *The Communist Manifesto* and, with Friedrich Engels, *Capital*. The evolutionary and transdisciplinary character of their arguments as well as their readiness to take conflict in society seriously can be seen as positive features of Marxist economics. On the negative side is the deterministic character of their arguments. History is interpreted in one specific way and the future must follow a predetermined pattern. Marxists mostly claimed to present a true theory in a monistic sense, but they also referred to their economics as 'political economy' which suggests a certain consciousness of the ideological character of their arguments.

The other line of thought which differs from the neo-classical one, is connected with the German Historical School in the 1840s and 1850s and later with the American Institutionalism of Thorstein Veblen and John R Commons. Scholars belonging to the Historical School argued in favour of inductive analysis based on empirical facts and were sceptical of abstract mathematical theory building based on assumptions that led to empty analysis or were unrealistic. Institutionalists like Thorstein Veblen shared the historical emphasis of the German Historical School and referred to economics in evolutionary terms. Veblen's transdisciplinary orientation is exemplified by his *Theory of the Leisure Class*. In this book, which appeared in 1899, he coined the term 'conspicuous consumption'. His analysis of a status aspect of consumption is very close to more recent attempts to account for 'status seekers'. Like the Marxists, Veblen was concerned about conflicts and power relationships in society but he also identified conflicts along other lines, for instance conflicts between innovating engineers in corporations and conservative capitalists as owners of production facilities.

As the term suggests, institutional economists tend to problematize 'institutional arrangements' in society rather than take them as given. The term 'institutional arrangements' is here used in a broad sense to include rules (formal and informal) as well as organization and power relationships. Among early writers, John R Commons took an interest in the fairness of the rules that regulate the labour market and the power of unions in relation to employers. Proposals of a reformist kind were presented to reduce confrontation (Rutherford, 1994).

Among economists who have more recently declared themselves institutionalists, K William Kapp and Gunnar Myrdal are of particular interest to this study. Kapp can be described as a precursor among environmental economists, with his book *The Social Cost of Private*

Enterprise (1950, 1971). Kapp pointed to the tendency in business to 'shift part of the costs of production to third persons and to the community as a whole' and argued that 'the original presumption against governmental regulation and the bias against planning which still pervades much of neo-classical value theory must be abandoned' (1970, p11).

> *In some cases, the social costs of production are felt immedi-ately; in other instances the ill effects of private production remain hidden for considerable periods of time, so that the injured persons do not become immediately aware of their losses. Furthermore, certain social losses affect only a limited group, whereas all members of society may feel others. Indeed, the actual damages caused by private productive activities may be distributed over so many persons that any one of them will individually sustain a relatively small loss. Although aware of his losses, the individual may not consider it worthwhile to take defensive action against the particular industrial concern responsible for his losses. In short, the term social cost refers to all those harmful consequences and damages which third persons or the community sustain as a result of the productive process, and for which private entrepreneurs are not easily held accountable* (Kapp, 1971, pp13–14).

Kapp was also sceptical of the idea of tackling environmental problems by placing monetary values on all kinds of impacts as in cost–benefit analysis. His ideas about approaches to decision-making and environmental policy are published in a number of articles. Some of these have since been compiled in book form by Ullman and Preiswerk in 1985 and Leipert and Steppacher in 1987.

Gunnar Myrdal's career as an economist began in the neo-classical camp. Myrdal wrote about price theory in the 1930s and became a prominent figure in the Stockholm School of Economics. A more active role for the government through investments in public works was recommended as a means of dealing with unemployment and other aspects of the Depression. In the USA, Thorstein Veblen was one of the men behind the New Deal policy, in England John Maynard Keynes had a similar role and in Sweden, members of the Stockholm School prepared and – as members of government – even implemented ideas of this kind.

While most economists in Sweden remained neo-classical, Myrdal's sensitivity to value issues and his transdisciplinary orientation made him diverge from the mainstream and declare himself an institutionalist. Transdisciplinary approaches are needed because of the impossibility of meaningfully demarcating some problems from others as being 'economic'. 'In reality, there are no 'economic', 'sociological', or 'psychological' problems, but just problems, and they are all complex' (Myrdal 1975, p142).

Institutionalists have their organizations too. Since 1966, there has been a US-based Association for Evolutionary Economics (AFEE) which publishes the *Journal of Economic Issues* and in 1989 a European Association for Evolutionary Political Economy (EAEPE) was formed in London. It may be noted that EAEPE has instituted two awards for young scholars, a Kapp Prize and a Myrdal Prize. Present-day institutionalism is perhaps best presented in a handbook edited by Hodgson et al (1994) which was produced by the co-operative efforts of representatives of the US-based and European associations. A review article by Warren Samuels (1995) can also be recommended.

The version of institutional economics that will be emphasized here can be characterized by its:

- emphasis on historical, evolutionary patterns of events (rather than equilibrium analysis);
- emphasis on relationships with biology, ecology and social sciences other than economics, and even to humanities rather than to traditional ideas about physics;
- tendency to be open-ended in its logic and its reliance at least in part, on fragmentary patterns and images (rather than closed mathematical models);
- view of 'institutions', defined as rules of the game, power relationships, resource endowments and organizational factors as important objects of study; and
- sensitivity to valuational and ideological issues.

Only the latter point on the value issues involved in social science research will be elaborated here, as it is so closely connected with the writings of Gunnar Myrdal:

> *Valuations are always with us. Disinterested research there has never been and can never be. Prior to answers there must be questions. There can be no view except from a viewpoint. In the questions raised and the viewpoint chosen, valuations are implied.*
>
> *Our valuations determine our approaches to a problem, the definition of our concepts, the choice of models, the selec-*

*tion of observations, the presentations of our conclusions –
in fact the whole pursuit of a study from beginning to end.
... In this context I have argued for, and in my own
research from an American Dilemma onward have tried to
observe, the necessity in any scientific undertaking of
stating, clearly and explicitly, the value principles which
are instrumental. They are needed not only for establishing
relevant facts but also for drawing policy conclusions*
(Myrdal, 1978, pp778–9).

In this quotation Myrdal speaks generally about 'values', 'valuations'
and 'value principles' while I tend also to refer to 'ideology' and
'ideological orientation' as defined in Chapter 1.

All articles, books and reports in economics are influenced by the
ideological orientation of the author and his or her particular socio-
cultural and institutional context. This book is no exception. Let us
take my previous story about the emergence of ecological economics
as an example. The story told can of course be checked with respect
to the facts by applying the intersubjectivity test. B, as an observer,
may agree with A that the ISEE conferences have been correctly
described with respect to time and place. But the positive tone of
presenting this ecological economics association and particularly the
European Chapter may not be shared by all. My story is organized in a
particular way, where value elements and factual elements together
suggest that ecological economics is a very promising field indeed.

Some of those who share my positive attitude to ISEE may nevertheless place their emphasis on other events and the role of other
individuals. They may argue, for instance, that the role attributed to
the Wallenberg Symposium in 1982 is exaggerated, that the 'story' has
other origins that are equally valid and legitimate, or that there is a
chauvinistic element in highlighting achievements by Swedish scholars
and organizations.

I can only agree with such criticisms in the sense that other stories
can be told about the evolution of the ecological economics movement
and that such stories may be of equal value, representing trustworthy
attempts to account for a series of events. This means that more than
one story may appear reasonable, stories that are similar in parts and
that differ in other parts. Presenting more than one story will elucidate the pattern of events in a more many-faceted way and the
differences between the stories told may be as interesting and thought
provoking as the similarities.

EPISTEMOLOGICAL TENSIONS AND COMPLEMENTARITIES

In his book *Development Betrayed. The End of Progress and a Coevolutionary Revisioning of the Future*, Richard Norgaard refers to a number of epistemological tensions in science (1994, p62). We will attempt to extend and elaborate on his list of epistemological tensions here (Table 2.1). Norgaard argued that the dominance of Cartesian ideals of good science (left hand part of the table) has led to many positive achievements but he also expressed the judgement that the limited understanding of alternate epistemological premises (right hand side) can explain some of the problems that we now face.

A preliminary distinction is made between 'mechanistic' and 'evolutionary' thinking: neo-classical economics tends to be mechanistic while institutional economics is on the evolutionary side. In neo-classical economics, the machine metaphor plays an important role with explanations given in terms of the 'forces' of 'supply' and 'demand' and the need to 'balance' such forces in equilibrium. Institutional economics, on the other hand, emphasizes patterns of events in historical time and in the study of possible future developments.

Table 2.1 *Epistemological Tensions within Economics and other Social Sciences*

Traditional premises	Complementary (or alternate) premises
Mechanistic	Evolutionary
Value neutrality	Values unavoidable
Objectivity	Subjectivity (interpretative)
Universal regularities	Contextualism, uniqueness, case studies
Reductionist	Holistic
One-directional causation	Multi-directional causation
Logically closed mathematical models	Pattern models that may be fragmentary
Optimal solutions	Illuminate, search consensus, mitigate conflicting interests
Disseminate knowledge	Interaction (dialogue and co-operative learning)

Neo-classical economists and many other scientists emphasize objectivity and value neutrality. This, as we have seen, is very different from Myrdal's ideas about the presence of values. Most scholars claim to have some freedom in choosing problems to work on, which perspectives or methods to apply and where to use these theories and methods. Research is supposed to differ from routine investigation and the scholar must choose where to search for this newness. The values that influence a scholar's work are, of course, a matter of her or his personality, the socio-cultural context in which he or she is working plus other aspects of the institutional context, power relationships included. The scholar may have ambitions to change her or his own situation or that of certain others and sometimes society at large. In trying to do so, the scholar's own ideological orientation, as well as the ideological or cultural atmosphere surrounding her or him, will play a role.

More recent writings about 'social constructivism' are relevant here, although those who present this view, like others who see themselves as 'scientists', appear reluctant to openly address the issues of values and power involved. The more common theme seems to be that the way a story about, for instance, some environmental problem is 'constructed', or designed, told and otherwise presented, will influence how the story is received by various groups of actors in society. Hannigan, for instance, discusses 'necessary factors for the successful construction of an environmental problem' (1995). He speaks about a claim-making process, the social construction of knowledge, communication and the role of the media and so on. In this respect, the discourse is not dissimilar to conventional business management literature about marketing or public relations activities. There seems to be the possibility to go further, however, and argue that conceptual frameworks are socially constructed by individuals and groups related to specific interests and power agglomerates.

Objectivity will continue to have a role, however, for instance when measuring the pH-value of water in a lake. But even in this case is it possible that someone will point to alternative theories and ways of measuring acidity. Objectivity can also be related to subjectivity (Table 2.1). Subjective and interpretative aspects are considered in phenomenology. Listening to various actors and interpreting their messages and points of view are important in 'narrative analysis' (Kohler Riessman, 1993). The stories told by individuals become as respected as other kinds of facts in our attempts to understand situations and processes. Donald McCloskey was perhaps the first to suggest that economics can be interpreted in this light (McCloskey, 1983). The presentation of central elements of neo-classical price theory – McCloskey's own speciality – is seen by him as a case of story telling. Why do economists like to tell this particular story about prices and markets rather than some other story? Why are they so eager to repeat the same story rather than something new? Here we are close to our previous discussion about social constructivism.

In the field of business studies, and organization theory in particular, interpretative studies are increasingly being used. An organization can be perceived as a complex and dynamic web of narratives (Czarniawska, 1997). In relation to environmental issues, listening to the actors involved may add to our knowledge and understanding of the limits to and possibilities for social change. We will return to this theme later as part of our discussion of the actor–network perspective.

Objectivity with an emphasis on a search for universal regularities or explanatory laws may still be worth pursuing, but it is argued here that uniqueness and contextualism are no less important (Table 2.1). In business management literature and other fields of social science, case studies have emerged as legitimate sources of knowledge.

Furthermore, an approach may be 'reductionist' or 'holistic'. Here, there seem to be two different interpretations of the opposite poles, one referring to the broadness of a concept or study, for instance 'micro' versus 'macro' in economics; the other concerning uni-dimensional versus multidimensional approaches or analyses. Taking one more example from economics, an institutionalist like myself regards neo-classical cost–benefit analysis as a case of 'monetary reductionism'. A holistic approach to decision-making, therefore, would be one where different kinds of impacts are kept separate. A disaggregated analysis in terms of 'impact profiles' is recommended.

Just as the relationship between individuals or actors is seen in interactional terms, our view of ecosystems or 'man-made systems' is conceptualized in multi-directional rather than uni-directional terms. One characteristic of 'systems thinking' is that all the components of a system interact and may in principle affect each other.

In neo-classical economics there is a preference for mathematical models, whereas institutionalists tend to speak of 'pattern models'. The latter rely primarily on a verbal language and pictures or images, that is visual patterns, which are regarded as no less relevant than numbers. Patterns may be fragmentary, reflecting uncertainty, rather than complete. It is argued that fragmentary patterns can often be meaningful to the observer.

For many rather simple problems, mathematical techniques for finding optimal solutions could be relevant, for example in cases where there is no dispute about the objective function to be optimized and where quantification is meaningful. However, on the societal level, the situation is often much too complex for a simplistic mathematical treatment. Sensitivity to value issues and the imperatives of democracy become important and ideas about 'scientifically correct solutions' have to be replaced by more modest, but often more fruitful, attempts to 'illuminate' an issue. The role of the analyst is no longer that of dictating the 'correct' or 'optimal' solution as much as one of interacting with various actors and interested parties in a process of co-learning

(learning from each other) about values, possible options and impacts. Dialogue, negotiations, consensus building and conflict management are features of this differing approach to decisions. The traditional idea of the scientist or analyst as someone who can study a problem fairly independently, find solutions and disseminate his or her findings, is no longer valid.

PARADIGM CO-EXISTENCE RATHER THAN PARADIGM SHIFT

In an attempt to summarize our arguments from this chapter, I would like to return to the issue of pluralism. Monism versus pluralism can be discussed with respect to epistemology, paradigm and ideology/ ethics. These aspects are interrelated in the sense that the neo-classical paradigm is connected with certain epistemological ideas and principles and represents a specific ethical and ideological orientation. Similarly, the institutional paradigm can be interpreted with respect to epistemology and ideology/ethics.

Thomas Kuhn's ideas about 'paradigm shift' (Kuhn, 1970) are basically connected with monism. At any point in time, only one theory of science, paradigm is regarded as the correct one or as representing 'the truth'. Anomalies may appear at a certain stage in the sense that certain facts are seen as incompatible with the prevailing model. This in turn may lead to a search for a new explanatory model, which can accommodate the new facts. If such a model is discovered and accepted, it replaces the previous one and a 'paradigm shift' has occurred.

I think that this view of the world, where one paradigm completely replaces another and where only one perspective is seen as correct at any one time, has to be modified. Sometimes it is even a dangerous idea. It can lead to unnecessary confrontation in the scientific community and elsewhere, which may indeed hinder progress. Using economics as the example, neo-classicists who hear about institutionalism may become unnecessarily wary – even frightened. As part of a monistic view of science, only one paradigm can be correct: 'If they (the institutionalists) are right, we must be wrong. Since our knowledge has been shown to be useful in some areas, they must be wrong.'

Pluralism and 'paradigm co-existence' seems to me to be a much more fruitful basic principle. The philosopher Georg Henrik von Wright observes that there is a place for complementarity even in the natural sciences. Light as a phenomenon can be interpreted as part of a theory of particles, but also as part of a theory based on waves (von Wright, 1986). Each of the two perspectives – which are logically incompatible according to present knowledge – contributes to an understanding of light as a phenomenon. The wave theory adds to the understanding offered by the particles theory and vice versa. Relying exclusively on one of the two theories would limit our understanding of light as a phenomenon. Von Wright refers to Niels Bohr who argued that both models have to be accepted. They are at the same time both mutually exclusive and complementary. Bohr pointed to a number of examples and suggested a more general theory of the complementary aspects of reality.

Moving now to the social sciences, there are additional reasons for keeping an open mind. The history of economic thought or the history of sociology, psychology or political science over the last century suggests that there have always been competing perspectives. As already indicated, Marxist economics and institutionalism have played a role as alternatives to neo-classicism. Complementarity and paradigm co-existence seems to be a normal situation rather than an exception. An evolutionary perspective seems useful in understanding the history of economic ideas. Theories and paradigms are born and flourish for a time. They may survive or die away at some stage. The number of adherents to a particular paradigm may wax or wane between two points in time. This means that the idea of paradigm shift can still be used but only in a more limited sense of referring to a change in the 'dominant paradigm'. At a specific point in time, paradigm A may be the dominant one in relation to specific issues such as development and environment, or two paradigms, A and B, may be of equal importance in terms of adherents. Paradigms are sometimes modified or may merge with other paradigms, as suggested by Allan Randall, a neo-classical environmental economist:

> *The ultimate convergence of resource economists on the single true theory is an entirely false hope. The synthesis of the alternate schools of thought – a fond hope of many – is precluded for exactly the same reasons that preclude the climactic test (or series of tests) that eliminates all rival theories but one. Disagreement will be the norm, now and indefinitely, although the approximate foci of disagreement may change over time.*
>
> *It may be possible to misread this line of argument as implying that resource economics will be characterized, into the indefinite future, by endless disputes between institutionalists and neo-classicals with little change or progress in either paradigm and no generally applicable standards of excellence by which to make intraparadigm or cross-*

paradigm evaluations of particular contributions. To the contrary, there will be intraparadigm testing, leading to progress or degeneration in each paradigm. One or both schools may eventually be abandoned. Alternatively, paradigm shifts may occur as new evidence and novel arguments lead to abandonment of some avenues and expansion of others. Institutionalism or the neoclassical school (or both) may achieve a partial synthesis with some newly emerging and not incompatible paradigm. Excellence will be pursued ubiquitously. However, some dimensions of excellence are universal (logical rigour, for example), for other dimensions the standards of excellence will be internal to the paradigm (Randall, 1986, p213).

Our earlier emphasis on the role of values and on pluralism adds to the picture painted by Randall. Since economics is coloured by values and ideology, the only way of preventing economics from becoming a one-sided propaganda force in society is pluralism. Monism, in a social science which plays such a central role in public debate, can hardly be compatible with democracy. Or to put it more bluntly, relying exclusively on neo-classical economics in all parts of the world may even be comparable to the exclusive reference to Marxist economics in pre-1989 Eastern European economies. The breakdown of Soviet communism represents an important step forward, but market capitalism, which is now expanding rapidly towards globalization, tends to invoke ideological and paradigmatic monism rather than pluralism. As will be discussed later in this book, hope lies in democracy with its encouragement of open public debate.

Chapter 3

The Political Economic Person and the Political Economic Organization

The previous assertion that neo-classical economics is not enough leads to the following question: is it possible to 'socially construct' an economics that makes it possible to deal more fruitfully with environmental problems? An answer has already been suggested. It is possible to take steps toward the construction of an alternative economics with the help of alternative theoretical perspectives, such as institutional economics. Learning from theoretical perspectives in social sciences other than economics has also been recommended. In addition, listening to and participating in public debate on environmental and other development issues is a third source of ideas for the conceptual framework suggested here. The view that new knowledge comes exclusively from universities and research institutes is thereby rejected.

It has also been made clear that environmental problems of the kind addressed are largely caused by 'Man' (in a genderless sense) and that 'Man' also plays a significant role in attempting to solve the problems. Individuals who take their responsibility for nature and the environment seriously, or for their behaviour toward other individuals, are very important to this issue. As this fact should somehow be reflected in the world of theories and models for an alternative micro-economics, it is suggested that 'Man' should be regarded as a political being. Instead of, or in addition to, neo-classical Economic Man, a Political Economic Man/Woman is suggested; or to simplify our vocabulary, a Political Economic Person (PEP).

The idea is to make the individual more visible in our economic analysis, to make him or her someone who is described in holistic terms and in a way which allows for some degree of complexity. The naming of such a person could vary, as we are interested in the social and socio-psychological aspects of human behaviour and in cultural aspects as well. So instead of referring to PEP, we could have chosen another terminology, such as Socio-Economic Person, Social-Psychological Person, Socio-Cultural Person and perhaps even Socio-Biological Person, the latter terminology reflecting our biological characteristics – instincts related to territory being one example. We are intellectual and cultural beings in one sense, but the biological part cannot be overlooked. In the present approach, social, socio-psychological, cultural and biological aspects of human behaviour are all of importance. It is mainly our emphasis on 'Man' as a political being and potential actor that suggests that PEP is a preferable name. Ideology and ethics come to the forefront of our perceptions. It is assumed that 'Man' is guided by an 'ideological orientation'.

POLITICAL ECONOMIC PERSON

As already made clear, this book is an attempt to deal constructively with issues related to the environment and development. This means that policy at various levels, whether it be environmental policy or some other, is of primary importance. 'Policy' comes from somewhere and it is suggested that the individual in her or his different roles is a reasonable starting point. To reflect the political aspect of human behaviour, reference is made to a PEP.

Our Political Economic individual – what does she or he look like? Figure 3.1 is an attempt to single out some concepts that are of critical importance to an understanding of individuals in relation to environmental and other issues. At a basic level, reference will be made to roles, relationships, activities and motives or interests. Connected with specific roles are specific relationships, activities and motives/interests. At an integrating or coordinating level (cf 'integrating concepts' in Figure 3.1), all of the roles of the individual may be kept together under an 'identity', and all of the relationships of the individual may be referred to as a 'network'. The pattern of activities may be referred to as the 'life-style' of the individual. Finally, the motives/interests may be part of an 'ideological orientation'. Although my argument suggest some connection between roles and identity, between relationship and networks etc, this should not be taken too literally. 'Identity' may have an integrating function not only in relation to roles, but also for relationships, activities and motives/interests. Similarly, 'network' does not exclusively refer to the integration of relationships.

At any moment in time, the individual is positioned in relation to his or her environment and context. The individual's knowledge, power and other resources are essential when describing or understanding her or his 'position' in relation to a 'context' which can be

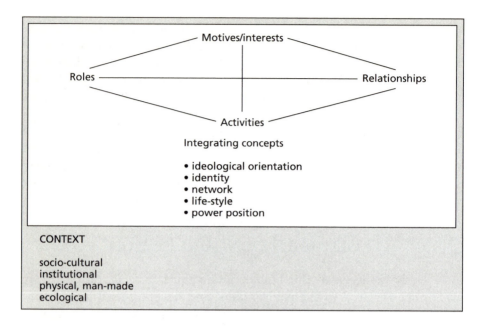

Figure 3.1 *Political Economic Person. Essential Concepts for an Understanding of a Person's Behaviour and Adaptation to her or his Context*

described as: 'socio-cultural', 'institutional', 'physical/man-made' and 'ecological'. The individual's behaviour and life-style are seen as an 'adaptation process' over time.

The conceptual framework outlined above will be elaborated below and at times comparison will be made to neo-classical Economic Man. It is assumed that for each individual, there is a set of relevant roles in relation to environmental and development issues, a set of relevant relationships, a set of relevant motives/interests and a set of relevant activities. Starting with the roles, it may be noted that neo-classical microeconomics emphasizes the role as consumer to the exclusion of almost all other roles. 'Man' also appears in another market-related role namely as wage-earner, or 'seller' of her or his labour. By selling labour, the individual obtains the money needed for consumption.

However, there are market-related roles less often discussed as part of neo-classical theory. Purchasing is not limited to ultimate consumption but is also a professional activity in business corporations. Moreover, some individuals act as investors, for instance in shares, and may prefer to invest in environmentally 'friendly' activities and corporations.

There is no dispute about the importance of the role of consumption (and other market-related roles) in relation to environment and development. (There are, however, different opinions about the relevance and sufficiency of the specific neo-classical approach to consumption; for an overview of alternative approaches, see Ackerman, 1997; Goodwin et al, 1997.) Connected with the role of consumer are purchasing and consumer activities, which in turn involve specific relationships to retail outlets or other entities where products (goods and services) are sold. Motives and interests may be connected with prices and other trading conditions. Our consumer may or may not consider 'green' labels as part of her or his 'ideological orientation' and decision-making.

But there are roles that are not primarily market-oriented, such as being a parent, a professional or a citizen. In relation to environmental and developmental issues, these 'non-market roles' can for some individuals be just as important as, or even more important than, the role of consumer. One person may be a worker who is concerned about environmental issues generally, and the work environment and other environmental performance of the production unit in particular, while another is a business leader and a third is a teacher. Even more 'private' roles, such as that of being a parent, may be of importance. Interaction between parent and child influences how each relates to the environment. In our roles as citizens, we are supposed to take an interest in societal issues of various kinds and environmental and development issues belong to this category.

Just as market related roles are connected with specific relationships, activities, motives and interests, the same can be said of non-market roles. As professionals, we 'belong to' or relate to specific organizations. We engage in specific activities and develop a set of relationships or a network, which in turn changes in specific ways with time. In the role of citizen, we may similarly take part in private and public debate in various 'arenas'. Specific activities and relationships are involved in this and through the interaction, we articulate and reassess our ideas about what is good for ourselves and society; that is our 'ideological orientation'.

While it can be useful to identify and discuss separate roles, it can be equally valuable to think of the individual as a 'whole person' with all of her or his different roles, relationships and interests. It is possible for one role to predominate or have 'spillover effects' in relation to other roles. Identity, life-style, world view and ideological orientation then become very much connected with the dominant role. One example that comes to my mind is the 'organic' or 'ecological' farmer. Most of those who take the step from conventional farming to ecological agriculture have 'internalized' a set of social and nature-related values in a way which not only influences their work, but their life-style as a whole. It is, of course, equally possible to find examples of how professional interests and activities can contribute to playing down or excluding environmental concerns from an individual's perceptions and agenda.

A SOCIO-PSYCHOLOGICAL FRAME OF REFERENCE

As already alluded to, the individual is seen as a 'social being', that is a person embedded in a web of social relationships. In spite of tensions between various motives and interests, the individual is somehow kept together by ideas of her or his role or identity in relation to each specific socio-cultural context. Dissonance theory, learning theories and other parts of social psychology are seen as relevant and useful in understanding behaviour. The individual strives for some congruence and balance between his or her roles, relationships, activities and interests, and may experience such balance, but incongruities and tensions also contribute to the characterization of human existence.

'Identity' refers to a person's 'self-image', her or his feelings of 'belonging'. The individual may simultaneously point to a professional 'homeness', the 'place' in geographical terms where she or he comes from or lives, her or his family or affiliation to a political party or ideology. Normally, there is a large degree of continuity in a person's identity ('self-sameness') – which is not to say that changes do not occur, especially over longer periods of time (Alsmark, 1997). The self-image of person A may differ more or less from some other person's, say B's, ideas about A's identity or 'belonging'. Similarly, there is a degree of continuity in a person's activity pattern over time which makes it meaningful to speak of her or his life-style. The recognition that one life-style may be much more wasteful than another with respect to degradation of natural resources and the health of human beings or of ecosystems, has made us realize that life-styles are an integral part of the problems faced.

Egoistic versus 'other-related' (for example community oriented) motives exemplify tensions that a person may experience. This points to a view of 'Man' as a 'moral being', where responsibility in relation to others and society at large becomes a potential issue. Amitai Etzioni, for example, has propounded an 'I & We Paradigm' (Etzioni, 1988), according to which the existence of a powerful ego in each healthy individual is not sufficient reason to denigrate or exclude the social and ethical aspects of human life. Each individual plays a part in many groups and organizations, or potential 'we-contexts', and such relationships involve a number of tensions and ethical issues. Ethics is equally relevant for 'we–they' relationships, for instance in situations of open conflict. Similarly, Amartya Sen, an open-minded, mainly neo-classical economist, has argued in favour of an explicit consideration of ethics, as opposed to what he sees as the 'engineering tradition' in economics (1987).

A comparison with neo-classical theory may be relevant here. The theory of the consumer is limited not only in the sense that one human role is emphasized at the expense of all others. In addition, consumer tastes and preferences are taken as given (and thereby treated as external to analysis). As part of an imagined value neutrality, the neo-classical scholar regards it as external to her or his role to problematize the values and life-styles of consumers. Each individual maximizes her or his own utility, whatever that means in ethical terms. But if, as many suggest, environmental problems are connected with present consumer tastes and life-styles and more generally with dominant world views in industrialized countries, then the neo-classical approach implies that essential aspects of the problems faced must be overlooked. The assumptions connected with Political Economic Person, where the 'ideological orientation' of the individual is seen as relevant, means that the different consumer preferences and life-styles of two individuals are no longer necessarily regarded as equally justified. Whether supported by a simultaneous, facilitating public policy or not, individuals may move in a step-by-step fashion away from lifestyles that are environmentally destructive toward those that are environmentally more beneficial. But again, whether such moves represent an advance is a matter of the ethical and ideological orientation of the observer. In my judgement, and in accordance with the Rio Declaration, getting closer to environmental sustainability represents such an advance.

The message of Adam Smith about 'the invisible hand' is subject to various interpretations but one common interpretation is that if one individual, A, emphasizes her or his own interests and does not bother too much about the interests of other individuals, B, C and D, or the interests of society at large, then she or he will nevertheless automatically do that which is best for society. This interpretation of the invisible hand idea simply legitimizes an unfettered egoism of individual A. To my way of thinking, neo-classical economics is very much founded on such assumptions about the negative outcome for everybody if a person starts to wonder about and problematize the ethical aspects of her or his behaviour. Contrary to this view, it is argued here that it is a move in the right direction if individual A, as part of her or his market transactions, carefully considers the implications for B, C, D and society at large. It is believed that a person who sometimes broadly considers the interests of others in her or his market behaviour will do a better job than someone who only maximizes her or his own utility or promotes her or his own interests. Similarly, if from one point in time to another, individual A succeeds in expanding her or his interests and concern for others and society at large, this is seen as a positive development.

It may be appropriate at this stage to reflect briefly on local activities being undertaken at the end of the 1990s in Sweden and many other countries along the lines of the Agenda 21 recommendations. When individuals as citizens and in all their other roles engage in these activities, this suggests a willingness to broaden or expand ethical concerns and responsibilities. What would a normally indoctrinated neo-classical economist say about such concerns and activities? In my judgement, their reasoning would be something like the above interpretation of Adam Smith, implying that attempts to internalize broader values are entirely misdirected. Just as neo-classical economists over the years have regarded environmentalists as 'strange fellows', this will also be the case with those who voluntarily and without immediate recompense take part in attempts to reorient the economy and society in an environmentally more friendly direction.

While neo-classicists tend to see individuals as robot-like optimizers who instantly react to price signals, institutionalists and many other social scientists point instead to the important role of habits in human behaviour. The individual is largely 'locked into' specific habits of thought and specific habitual activities that together form a pattern, here referred to as a life-style. At an early stage, Herbert Simon pointed to selective perception, limited cognitive capacity and search costs as relevant to an understanding of human behaviour (Simon, 1945). As humans beings we tend to stick to familiar environments and use various rules of thumb to deal with complexity. When seen from the outside, the development of a habit can be expressed in terms of increases in the probability of a specific behaviour (such as purchasing a specific brand, K, of coffee among available alternatives K, L and M) for successive trials (ie purchasing situations of a similar kind, cf Howard, 1963). This emphasis on habitual behaviour does not, however, exclude the possibility of 'problemistic search' and conscious decision-making. At times the individual perceives a problem and alternative courses of action. Habits are reconsidered and behaviour may change.

Our PEP is therefore a complex figure. On the one hand, there is a strong tendency for habitual behaviour and inertia with respect to life-style; on the other hand the possibility of conscious decision-making. As a result of external pressure (a change in context, see Figure 3.1) and/or own initiative, the individual may change her or his behaviour. Before taking a decision, individual A may, as part of her or his ideological orientation, consider non-monetary as well as monetary impacts upon various affected parties or stakeholders. Individual A then becomes an actor who refers to an 'ideological orientation' as a more or less fragmentary map in an attempt to adapt to an unchanged or changing environment.

IDEOLOGICAL ORIENTATION AS A KEY CONCEPT

Though fundamental, the socio-psychological frame of reference indicated is still not enough. Another characteristic of our PEP is her or his 'ideological orientation'. As previously defined, 'ideology' refers to 'ideas about means and ends' in relation to specific spheres of human activity. A person's ideological orientation rests on beliefs and is perceived by the person as more or less uncertain. This hypothetical and uncertain nature is one reason for using the term 'ideological orientation', rather than ideology.

'Ideological orientation', therefore, refers to a mindset characterized by often fragmentary patterns of seeing, thinking and feeling and is very different from the complete, logically closed, mathematical objective function assumed in neo-classical analysis. Ideas and images are essential elements in the ideological orientation of an actor and these ideas and images change as a result of partly unconscious, partly conscious, processes. Changes in such ideas and images are furthermore hindered or facilitated by various contextual factors, for instance by the interested parties involved and by the institutional arrangements related to an issue.

Science and public debate play a role by influencing ideas and images, that is the ideological orientation of individual actors and citizens. These ideas and images can be seen, at least in part, as socially constructed to achieve specific purposes. As an example, the ideas and images of textbooks in economics and business management may influence the views that students and other actors hold about 'Man', 'Man–Nature' relationships, economics, efficiency, development, social change and about various institutions, such as the business corporation, the market, the state and so on.

For the habitual part of a person's behaviour, it is assumed that the ideological orientation furnishes guidance in the form of rules of thumb. The ideological orientation also serves the function of valuing various phenomena as part of a person's more conscious adaptations to her or his context. There is a valuational and emotional aspect of our attitudes to various objects or persons and more generally to our environment, but valuation may also refer to past, ongoing and future

activities, projects and policies. Since this issue of valuation is fundamental to our ideas on rationality, economics and efficiency, I will
elaborate on it briefly.

As part of neo-classical economics, it is normally implied that
rationality and decision-making have to do with the maximization
(minimization) of an objective function. Examples include the
consumer who is assumed to maximize utility and the firm which
maximizes monetary profits. The cost–benefit analyst similarly
maximizes 'present value' at a societal level, where 'value' refers to
pecuniary or monetary. value as expressed by a set of actual or
'shadow' prices. While not excluding the usefulness of optimization
in mathematical terms for some subset of decision-making situations,
it is suggested here that 'rationality' and decision-making are based
primarily on ideology and ethics, that is a person's 'ideological orientation'. Individuals appear in specific roles and contexts and make
conscious decisions as part of adaptation processes, where 'orientation', 'profile', 'compatibility', 'matching' and 'pattern recognition'
are key concepts.

One of our strengths as human beings is our ability to recognize
patterns (Simon, 1983). Decisions can be thought of in terms of
matching the multifaceted and multidimensional ideological orientation or profile of each decision maker with the similarly multifaceted
and multidimensional impact profile of each alternative (Figure 3.2).
This view opens the way for multidimensional thinking and visualizing
in terms of pictures or 'Gestalts' in addition to one-dimensional
numbers. According to this view, an alternative is attractive to an
individual if a 'good fit' between her or his ideological orientation and
the impact profile of the alternative considered is expected or experi-
enced. As part of a conscious decision process, individuals may
reconsider their ideological orientation. In this sense, the values, or
even the principles of valuation, are not seen as constant and given,
but may change as part of the learning processes of and dialogue
between the actors involved.

To illustrate this idea of viewing the relationship between the
decision maker(s) and each alternative considered in terms of a
'pattern recognition' or 'matching' process, an example from private
life may be of help. Complex decision situations exist not only in
organizations and in public life but also, as most of us have realized,
in the realm of our private affairs. Let us assume that the members of a
family have taken a decision to relocate and buy a new house. A
number of options are being considered. Each family member is
assumed to refer to an ideological orientation, in this case an idea of
what might constitute a 'good', 'satisfactory' or even the 'best' solution

Figure 3.2 *A Holistic Idea of Rationality and the Decision Act. The Ideological Profile of each Decision Maker is Matched against the Expected Impact Profile of each Alternative*

to the problem faced. When visiting one of the houses considered in its specific context and when learning about its functional, aesthetic and other qualities, each member might test the compatibility between her or his image(s) and other ideas of a good solution and her or his expectations of the impacts of the particular alternative at hand. If all the family members experience a 'good fit', then they may be ready to make the purchase – or may decide to continue the search in the hope of finding an even better alternative.

Whether applied at the level of private or public affairs, or something in between, the above idea of rationality does allow for pictures and images, that is visual cognitive processes, in addition to quantitative measurement and analysis, for instance of monetary cost or physical space. Numbers of the latter kind never represent more than a partial analysis and should be regarded as elements in an overall picture, which also includes qualitative descriptions and images. There are systematic approaches to decision-making other than those ending with one-dimensional numbers and experiences from private life suggest that individuals often prefer the holistic or non-reductionist idea of rationality indicated here.

In his book *A Primer in Decision Making*, James March makes a similar distinction between two approaches to decision-making, one in terms of optimization and the other as a matter of 'appropriateness'. Decision makers may 'pursue a logic of appropriateness, fulfilling identities or roles by recognizing situations and following rules that match appropriate behaviour to situations they encounter' (March, 1994, pviii).

POLITICAL ECONOMIC RELATIONSHIPS

Our political economics approach started with the PEP. We will now continue by interpreting relationships between individuals in similar terms. Some relationships can be described as being market relationships while other relationships are of a non-market character, for instance administrative relationships within an organization or more private relationships between individuals. All these kinds of relationships – and even those with a strong market component – will be interpreted in political terms. Any idea that markets are opposed to politics is thereby rejected. As a next step, the political role of organizations will be dealt with. Reference will therefore be made not only to Political Economic Relationships, but also to Political Economic Organizations (PEOs). The fact that many business organizations today refer to their 'environmental policy', suggests that it is appropriate to refer to a business corporation in political terms.

All kinds of relationships between actors are potentially important to an understanding of environmental policy issues and environmental performance. Public and private debate may be as relevant as market relationships or relationships within an organization. And not all organizations are business companies as exemplified by universities and environmental organizations. What transpires at universities, or among intellectuals more generally, may be as decisive for the sustainability issue as anything else.

Individuals with their roles, activities and ideological orientation relate to each other as suggested by Figure 3.3. When compared with the previous view of PEP in Figure 3.1, 'resources' and 'power' are emphasized as essential for an understanding of interaction between actors as part of a relationship. Resources and power in turn have to do with the know-how and goodwill of an actor and her or his control over property of various kinds, for instance financial and physical property.

The importance of public and private debate is emphasized here since it is more or less neglected in neo-classical theory. Neo-classical discourse – if there is any at all – tends to be limited to markets and prices. To interpret relationships in terms of price signalling is rather meagre in relation to many real-world situations. Figure 3.3 should be understood as a general model of relationships, whereas a market relationship becomes one, admittedly important, special case. For a market relationship 'Actor A' is replaced by 'Market Actor A' and 'Actor B' by 'Market Actor B' in Figure 3.3. Also when referring to markets, a broad frame of reference is needed. Remember Alfred Hirschman, the economist who became known for his rather trivial observation that in addition to 'exit' (in the sense of 'withdrawal from a market relationship'), there is 'voice' (meaning that actors can speak to each other) as an option in communication and attempts to influence a company or other market actor (Hirschman, 1970).

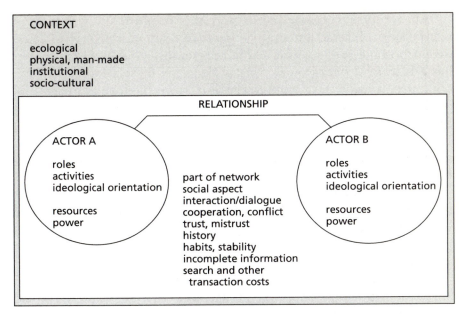

Figure 3.3 *Essential Aspects of a Relationship between two Actors*

As suggested by Figure 3.3, a relationship is normally part of a larger network where individuals as actors are linked to one another. Understanding a relationship between actors A and B will often be facilitated by studying other relationships and networks that A is involved in and other relationships and networks that B is involved in. What can be done in terms of developing a specific relationship according to some ideological orientation (for instance in a 'green' direction) is usually facilitated or hindered by a number of other relationships that the two actors are part of.

The social (and even emotional) aspect of a relationship is often important, even in the case of market relationships. A division within ABB (Asea Brown Boveri) has relationships with a specific number of suppliers and on both sides individuals are involved. They interact and engage in a dialogue in their attempts to improve the performance of both companies (Figure 3.3). Ideas about the market as a place where people meet anonymously appear reasonable only in some special cases, such as markets for currencies.

Some relationships are co-operative relationships built on trust, while others are better characterized in terms of conflict and mistrust. Actors A and B may disagree in ideological terms about environmental issues, for example. Interaction and dialogue between the two may lead to an aggravated conflict – or represent a step toward improved mutual understanding.

All actors have their habits and this is normally reflected in relationships. Interaction and co-operative relationships may to some extent become routine. Just as each person involved in a relationship has a historical background, this is also true of relationships. Each relationship has a development pattern, from birth to maturity and perhaps decay. Finally, contrary to the assumptions made in neo-classical theory, incomplete information on the part of each actor is a normal state of affairs. In the case of ABB mentioned above, moving from one supplier to another will in most cases involve search costs as well as other transaction costs.

Figure 3.3 also suggests that no relationship should be seen in isolation. In addition to a network of relationships, there is a broader socio-cultural context as well as a range of institutional arrangements in the form of laws and other rules of the game. Furthermore, there is a man-made, physical infrastructure and a biological context in the form of ecosystems. In fact, ecosystems too can be seen as a kind of infrastructure, as they supply goods and services to individuals. As part of this attempt to manipulate the perceptions of my readers, building a road no longer necessarily means that the existing infrastructure is enlarged or improved, but rather that one kind of infrastructure is replaced by another.

The importance of relationships and networks is emphasized elsewhere, for instance in the business management literature. In the study of industrial markets, illustrations can be found that in important respects are similar to Figure 3.3. An 'interaction approach' is emphasized in a book entitled *Understanding Business Markets. Interaction, Relationships, Networks* published by the Industrial Marketing and Purchasing Group at the Department of Business Studies, Uppsala University (Ford, 1990, see the illustration of relationship on page 20). The title of a later book *Developing Relationships in Business Networks* (Håkansson and Snehota, 1995) points in the same direction. While many of the aspects of relationships mentioned here are similar to those found in studies of industrial markets, there are also some important differences. The studies of industrial markets referred to are carried out primarily at company level, that is, the companies are in most cases seen as the 'actors'. Individuals as actors may appear, but are less visible than they are in the frame of reference suggested here.

The term 'environment' in the studies by Håkansson and his colleagues refers to market structure, position in the marketing channel and internationalization, and not to the kind of 'environment' discussed in this book. Value or ethical issues are largely avoided and private roles and individuals' roles as citizens are not discussed. No reference is made to 'life-style', 'ideological orientation' or similar concepts. But many of the 'soft' variables are there, such as the 'image' of a corporation or its 'goodwill' in relation to customers. In spite of the differences mentioned, our approach and that of the Uppsala group appear to be, in the main, mutually supportive and compatible.

THE ORGANIZATION AND ITS STAKEHOLDERS

In neo-classical microeconomics, the kind of organization recognized is the profit maximizing firm. While being useful for some purposes, this model of organizations does not meet our present demands, or to put it in different terms, is not compatible with the 'ideological orientation' of this book:

- The theory of the firm reduces all kinds of organizations to a single model (or alternatively does not claim to cover organizations that do not fit into the model).
- The theory of the firm furthermore aggregates or reduces all kinds of interests related to an organization to one objective function, which is maximized.
- Impacts that are multidimensional are reduced to one monetary dimension, thereby hiding multidimensional realities.
- Individuals are rendered invisible.
- Issues of ideology, ethics, participation and responsibility are not raised.

In relation to environment and development issues, these features of the neo-classical model become problematic. Most of us realize that not only business organizations have to be considered but also some other (if not all) kinds of organizations – citizen environmental organizations (CeO), religious organizations, universities and so on – as part of a public debate. Efficiency in energy terms or in materials handling is a concern for all organizations.

Actors who take part in the debate about environment and development have very different interests. Vested interests and differing views about ideology suggest that a conflict perspective is relevant in many cases and perhaps even as the normal case. The monetary dimension is of importance in almost all organizations, but monetary analysis of profits is normally understood here as partial analysis. In business and elsewhere, 'eco-efficiency' is increasingly regarded as an issue per se. 'Environmental auditing' and 'reporting' suggest that some stakeholders do not regard monetary auditing and reporting as sufficient.

The theory of the firm focuses on commodities, production costs and on revenues from commodity sales. Complexities of social life within the organization and in its 'external' relations, issues of leadership, labour unions and so on, are not dealt with. The theory does not raise issues of ideology but instead dictates that a special kind of optimization, understood as profit maximization in some sense, is the correct ideology.

In the business management literature, steps have been taken to overcome some of the above limitations of the theory of the firm. Organization theorists have introduced a stakeholder model of the firm and of other organizations. In relation to a specific organization, an attempt is made to identify all interested parties, that is all those who have something 'at stake' in relation to the functioning and performance of the organization. Employees, shareholders, other investors, suppliers, customers, neighbours (who may suffer from pollution, for example) are among the interest groups normally identified.

In our view, a move from the neo-classical theory of the firm to a stakeholder model is a significant step. Having something at stake can be based on ownership, but may also be based on other contractual relationships (such as employment) and on non-contractual relationships (connected with pollution from a factory) with an organization. Stakeholders may be related to the total activities of an organization or to specific decision situations characterized by a specific set of alternatives of choice. In the latter case, those who will be affected differently, depending on the option chosen, may be called stakeholders or interested parties in relation to the decision situation. But the meaning of being 'affected differently' can of course vary. A person may be 'concerned' about an issue such as a proposal to close a factory in some specific location. These citizens can be called 'stakeholders' in a broader sense of the concept. As a citizen one has the right to an opinion on such issues and, as we all know, prevailing ideas about democracy encourage individuals to raise their voices.

The stakeholder model represents a break with the monistic, equilibrium thinking of the neo-classical theory of the firm, for instance by suggesting that the interested parties related to an organization may have conflicting interests. The role of the chief executive is described as a mediator or broker who attempts to reconcile all the different interests, to find a reasonable balance, which is acceptable to all parties. Non-market relationships and non-monetary dimensions (eg pollution) are furthermore taken into account to some extent.

But there are also limits to the stakeholder model. In illustrations of the stakeholder model of organizations, there is a tendency to place equal weight on all stakeholder categories. Little is said about differences in power between actor categories. In a business corporation, shareholders have a special role as principals. Some subsets of the shareholders are represented on the board and, together with the chief executive, will influence the kind of balance that emerges between different interests. Other stakeholders may also have power of specific kinds and in varying degrees. Qualitative differences between the rights and power of different stakeholder categories appear to be very important.

It is furthermore generally assumed that there is a homogeneity of interests within each stakeholder category, at least if one is to believe the way the stakeholder model is illustrated. Very little is said for instance about possible differences between shareholders in the same corporation. Most people realize that there is a big difference in the power associated with share holdings between small owners and those who own large blocks of shares. But not so many people realize that the assumption generally made about the objectives of shareholders may not always reflect reality. For some, increases in dividends and in the market value of shares is the sole consideration, while for others there may also be an issue of 'ideological orientation'; not only monetary but also ethical considerations and environmental performance are relevant to some shareholders. This category of shareholders may increase or decrease in number over time.

If there is some heterogeneity among shareholders in a small company or in a transnational corporation with respect to ideological orientation, it becomes relevant to ask how much the managers of a corporation know about the ideological orientation of different shareholders in relation to environmental issues generally, or specific environmental issues. A second question is: do the managers want to know? Or, do they prefer to rely on a reductionist idea of value and efficiency, largely legitimized by neo-classical economics and much business literature? If shareholders are not completely different from citizens at large, one can expect that the number of 'green' shareholders (in some sense) is increasing over time. How is this reflected in the thinking and behaviour of leading actors in the corporation?

There are many points of discussion in relation to the stakeholder model. One and the same individual may appear in more than one stakeholder category and exert her or his influence. The chief executives are not always appropriately described as 'mediators'. They are themselves stakeholders and too often, it seems, use their position and influence to increase their own wealth. Even when they fail in their executive role and lose their jobs, they expect (and often receive) generous 'compensation'.

The debate about the stakeholder model does not end, however, with the arguments presented here. It has been argued, for instance, that thinking in terms of stakeholders should not be limited to business corporations but could be used to modify our view of the economy as a whole (Biesecker et al, 1998). It represents a way out of the fixation on property ownership and points to more general rights of citizens to participate in and influence the development process in a region or a country. As an example, it might be a good idea to start with a specific individual (rather than an organization) in an attempt to identify and illustrate stakeholder relationships. Most individuals are associated with a large number of organizations of both market and non-market kinds and may in addition be involved in numerous other issues. The person is thus an interested party or stakeholder and may have more or less power to influence future developments as part of each specific interest or stakeholder relation.

A POLITICAL ECONOMICS VIEW OF ORGANIZATIONS AND MARKETS

While having certain strengths, the stakeholder model does not contribute very much in terms of raising ideological issues. An attempt to overcome this weakness will be made here by referring to 'political economic organizations'. An organization is regarded as a collectivity of individuals. Our Political Economic Organization (PEO) model is built on PEP assumptions, where the individual is seen as an actor (Söderbaum, 1999b). The organization is regarded as 'polycentric' in the sense that each actor has her or his specific ideological orientation, which in relation to work may differ more or less from the ideological orientation or 'business concept' of the organization as a collectivity. In this way, we try to ensure that our PEP is not completely engulfed by the organization.

It is a trivial observation that when an organization such as a business corporation or a university moves in a 'green' direction, not all actors or stakeholders connected with that organization change their minds at the same time, in the same way or to the same degree. Some may act as 'entrepreneurs' in environmental affairs, taking initiatives of various kinds and encouraging others to participate in a process of change. At a specific moment in time, some actors in the employee category may be 'green' in orientation, while others are not. Similarly, some shareholders in the company may prefer a 'green' orientation and strategy for the company, while other shareholders are less concerned. In this way, 'green' employees, 'green' shareholders, 'green' suppliers, 'green' customers, 'green' investors have something in common – their ideological orientation. Similarly, actors belonging to the 'non-green' category have something in common, and this may represent a potential force in influencing the change (or lack of change) process of the company. Changes in the business concept or profile of an organization usually cause tensions. Individuals connected with specific actor categories in one network may differ in their views from those of another network and each actor within such networks may exert her or his power to influence the course of events.

Markets can similarly be seen in the light of polycentric networks of individuals as actors. The idea is simple. For example 'green' consumers will prefer 'green' producers or companies. 'Green' producers in turn will look for 'green' suppliers, and so on. Market segmentation along 'green' lines will occur and 'green' networks will compete with those that are 'less green' or 'non-green'. As suggested by the Uppsala school, a relationship between one customer and one supplier can sometimes be seen as an 'organization' of its own, in the sense that the two market actors enter into technological or other forms of co-operation. In this case the boundary between the two organizations may become less clear.

Reasoning in terms of ideological orientation, business concepts and mission statements leads to a conditional view of the functioning of organizations and markets. Some scholars and 'practical men' have a very optimistic idea of organizations, such as transnational corporations, or of the market. All problems, environmental problems included, will be solved by the invisible hand. Others, such as David Korten (1995), warn against this kind of dogmatism. The 'conditional view' advocated here simply states that the functioning of organizations and markets depends to a large extent on individuals as actors in organizations and market places, on their knowledge, and on their moral and ideological orientation. Certainly the rules of the game and other elements of the institutional context are also important. And the rules of the game are not only a matter of prevailing laws and guidelines at the national level. The actors themselves can exert an influence on the system of laws and even create their own rules. The rules formed as part of the 'self-regulation' of business may be less permissive than those implemented through the state. To comply with existing laws is no longer enough for many companies.

Finally it may be added that our reasoning in terms of actors and networks also leads to criticism of neo-classical public choice theory, or perhaps to a modified version of this theory. Neo-classical public choice theory can be described as a theory that refers to broad, mainly professional, categories of individuals in society, for instance farmers, bureaucrats and politicians (Mueller, 1979). Social change is seen in terms of a power game, involving lobbying, negotiation and other 'rent-seeking' activities at the national level. It is a theory which claims to predict which interest groups are likely to succeed or fail in the struggle for a bigger share of the cake. (One may think of it as a kind of stakeholder model on a national level, with the exception that issues of power, manipulation and tactical behaviour are much more openly addressed.) Rather than egoism at the individual level, public choice theory assumes (and thereby legitimizes, one may add) a kind of 'collective egoism' connected with each identified actor category or interest group. Farmers are assumed to maximize their incomes and shares of the total cake (gross domestic product or income) and not to bother much about broader societal interests or solidarity between groups. Bureaucrats similarly maximize their power by increasing their budgets and their incomes. Politicians are assumed to maximize their votes.

On this basis, it is predicted that interest categories that are small in number relative to the total population in a country, stand a better chance of keeping their group together and succeeding in lobbying activities. In this way farmers, numerically a relatively small group in each country, are expected to be successful, expectations that are supported by empirical observations about subsidies to farming, and so on. Environmental interests, perhaps, represent the opposite extreme (Olson, 1982). They are more dispersed in the total population and cannot be so easily formulated. They therefore tend to lose ground when compared with the well-defined interests of farmers.

However, the ideas of farmers (or bureaucrats) as forming a unified category can be questioned (Söderbaum, 1991, 1992, see also Chapter 7 on public choice and actor–network models of social change). When 'ideological orientation' is taken into account – and not only in the more obvious case of politicians, but as a general phenomenon – the predictions of public choice theory become more dubious or shaky. As an example, it becomes unrealistic to regard farmers (or bureaucrats) as a homogeneous category. We know that some farmers are engaged in 'ecological farming' and are 'green' in this sense, while others are less concerned about environmental issues or even tend to deny that any problems exist. Green farmers may find that they have interests in common and work together. Their interests will differ somewhat from 'non-green' farmers. In addition, 'green' farmers may find that they have interests in common with 'green' actors belonging to other actor categories, such as 'green' bureaucrats and may engage along with them in network building and lobbying activities. Along these lines, predictions made on the basis of the assumptions of conventional public choice theory (Olson, 1982, pp33–4) – for instance about the pale future of environmental interests – are not necessarily well grounded. Ideology and 'ideological competition' between individuals, organizations and networks can be as important, or more important, than the collective egoism, which is a distinctive feature of neo-classical public choice theory.

Chapter 4

Economics, Efficiency and Ideological Orientation

Most people have some ideas about the meaning of words such as 'economics', 'efficiency', 'rationality'. Where do these ideas come from? Everyday talk with friends and colleagues is one possible answer; reading newspapers, listening to the radio and watching television represent other possibilities. Some get their ideas from studying 'economics' at school or at university, or perhaps through distance tuition courses, which are becoming increasingly popular.

Somewhere behind all this are textbooks in economics and the business management literature. And education is somehow related to the research that goes on in these areas. Definitions of 'economics' in textbooks are certainly influential. If economists at universities agree about specific definitions of economics and of efficiency, then this will probably influence various actors or 'practical men', to use the language of Keynes cited earlier. If, on the other hand, economists disagree about these matters, then many more definitions will circulate among people and influential actors.

Traditional ideas about science lead us to expect that economists should agree in the name of 'truth' and 'clarity' about how to define 'economics', 'efficiency' and 'rationality'. These ideas about having one definition or paradigm at a time, with the possibility of 'paradigm-shift' under exceptional circumstances, do not to fit well with, or are not well adapted to, the social sciences. Our earlier reasoning pointed instead in the direction of pluralism and 'paradigm-coexistence', which means that more than one definition of economics should be accepted or even encouraged. It was argued that each definition reflects or is coloured by values and ideology. Reducing all possible definitions and thereby ideological orientations to one, would mean that science dictates what the correct ideology should be. Unfortunately, in the case of economics, science tends to play just such a role by limiting public debate and democracy in this respect. Fortunately, one may add, ordinary people think for themselves and do not always heed what economists say.

There appear to be two ways out of this quandary. First, no definition can claim 'exclusive rights'. Neo-classical definitions need not be abandoned, but monopoly claims by neo-classical authors to define economics need to be rejected. Given the ideological content of each definition, pluralism and paradigm coexistence is the only reasonable position. Secondly, each author has to choose a definition that is compatible with her or his ideological orientation and view of the problems faced. In relation to environmental and development issues, which are our present concern, one may look for a conceptual framework that helps us understand what is currently happening and what is helpful in seeing, identifying and dealing with the problems. The idea that one definition of economics and one conceptual framework is useful for all kinds of problems is thereby abandoned.

THE 'MONETARY REDUCTIONISM' OF NEO-CLASSICAL ECONOMICS

A view often put forward is that 'economics is about money'. 'It is about how to make money or profits'. This view has some support in neo-classical economics, where 'economics' is normally defined as 'management of scarce resources'. As part of this view, it is usually observed that there are many kinds of resources – financial resources, physical man-made resources like factories and machinery, human resources and natural resources, the latter here exemplified by land, minerals, forests and fish. Dealing with all these kinds of resources as they are becomes too complex, it is argued. Some kind of 'common yardstick' is needed and money is normally suggested as the 'natural' solution to this problem. So, 'resource allocation' tends to be dealt with largely, if not exclusively, in monetary terms. What is initially seen as a multidimensional phenomenon is reduced to monetary analysis. Prices in monetary terms are used in the process and it is argued that this is a very 'rational' way of approaching most, if not all problems.

Investment decisions lie at the heart of neo-classical analysis and, in the case of the firm, money should be allocated to obtain the best possible return, or profit. At the societal level, that project, or portfolio of projects should be chosen, which maximizes 'present value'. The emphasis on 'economic growth' in terms of gross domestic product (GDP) at the societal level is part of the same ideology. In this case too, 'net value added' in monetary terms is maximized.

The arguments put forward in favour of the kind of 'monetary reductionism' indicated here are numerous. As one example, it is argued that science invariably involves simplifying assumptions and that one has to do something to make a complex situation tractable. It is furthermore explained that politicians and other decision makers need simple answers to complex problems.

The 'appropriate' level of simplification for specific categories of decision makers can be discussed at length and we will return to these issues later. One may ask what will be lost, for instance, in terms of relevance for environmental or other specific categories of problems by reducing all impacts to a monetary dimension? More important for the time being is that the monetary reductionism of neo-classical theory is not only specific in conceptual terms, but also in ideological terms.

As an example of this simultaneous reductionism in ideological terms, 'value' is always defined as 'monetary value'. In environmental economics textbooks, for example David Pearce (Pearce et al, 1989, p62) has defined 'total economic value' for purposes of valuation at the societal level as follows:

Total Economic Value = Actual Use Value + Option Value + Existence Value

Let us choose the case of a forest, rich with various species, where a specific project involving logging activities has been proposed. The two alternatives, of preserving the forest or of exploiting it, can be compared according to the above equation. The forest in its present state can be used for recreational purposes, for instance, and there are certain methods neo-classical economists can refer to in order to estimate the monetary value of such usage. (These methods include the 'hedonic price approach', the 'contingent valuation method' and the 'travel cost approach'.) The alternative of cutting down the forest will provide 'use values' in terms of net incomes for the logging company when the timber is sold. In addition there are 'option values', that is the monetary value of having the options at some later point in time of preserving or cutting the forest or using it for some other purpose. 'Existence values' refer to 'the existence of whales, a value unrelated to use' (ibid, p61). In our case of the forest, there may be a species which is threatened by the logging activities and the monetary value of these species as well as the probability of their extinction have to be considered.

We will not go into detail about this here. Neo-classical economists themselves realize that there are some methodological problems with the approaches indicated. They may understand the difficulties or even impossibility of meaningfully estimating 'option values' and 'existence values' in monetary terms. They nevertheless stick to the idea, or I would say illusion, of monetary valuation. The alternative of giving up the idea of a monetary calculation at the level of all impacts does not seem to have been considered and other issues about paradigms and ideology are largely avoided.

In my judgement, the neo-classical cost–benefit project is heroic, especially in relation to environmental and development issues. The approach is characterized by reductionism in four respects:

1   reductionism in kind (all kinds of impact are reduced to one – monetary – kind of impact);
2   reductionism in space (impacts at different places are made comparable or 'tradable');
3   reductionism with respect to the interests affected (all kinds of impacts on all kinds of interests or groups of individuals are made 'tradable');
4   reductionism in time (impacts at different points in time are reduced to impacts at one point in time).

In this extreme version of a market ideology, there are no limits to the possibilities of trading impacts against each other. When comparing alternatives, complex patterns of impacts of various kinds at different points in time, at different localities and in relation to different groups of individuals or ecosystems, are easily brought together in a single monetary value (a 'present value') referring to one point in time. All possible ideological orientations are reduced to a specific version of a market ideology and we are all expected to take this seriously.

When it is understood that neo-classical economics is specific also in ideological terms in the sense that all other ethical and ideological approaches are excluded, then the following questions can be raised: is this particular conceptual framework and ideology a fruitful one for our attempts to deal constructively with environmental and development problems? Do the analysts or 'experts' really know what they are doing when reducing a multidimensional complexity to some alleged monetary equivalent? Do the politicians understand – or do they not need to understand – what they are doing when relying on the calculations of a particular analyst? Can we all agree about this conceptual and ideological approach, or should we look for alternative or complementary possibilities? Is there perhaps an 'ideological demand' for alternative conceptual and ideological frameworks? Since, in my opinion, science cannot and should not dictate the 'correct' ideology for society, we should perhaps respond to such demands in an open-minded way by supplying other conceptual frameworks that have a different ideological content.

SOME OBSERVATIONS FROM THE WORLDS OF POLITICS AND BUSINESS

Some steps have been taken in the last few decades to counteract the dominance of monetary thinking in relation to environmental issues. Examples are the institutionalization and increased use of environmental impact assessment (EIA) and environmental impact statements (EIS) as processes and documents, and the increasing use of life-cycle analysis (LCA) in business and other organizations. More generally, a number of standardized Environmental Management Systems (EMS) such as EMAS and ISO 14000 have been established for business and other organizations. Let us take a look at these new tools and their significance for our ideas about economics.

In the late 1960s and early1970s, it became increasingly obvious in the USA that when important investment decisions concerning utilities, roads, airports, etc were made by governmental agencies, environmental impacts tended to play a minor and secondary role when compared with financial and technical considerations. As part of the 1969 National Environmental Policy Act (NEPA), rules and guidelines were agreed upon for EIA as a process and for the content of EISs as a product and document. A governmental agency that proposed a project, such as a dam and hydroelectric plant, had to carefully estimate the environmental impacts of the proposed action. It also had to carefully investigate whether, by modifying the project, it would be possible to mitigate environmental impacts and explore whether there were alternatives to the proposed project that would entail less serious impacts on ecosystems. In addition to demands on the quality of documentation and the final EIS, there are rules about participation in the decision-making process. According to the US system, it is also possible to go to court, with the argument that, for instance, alternatives to the proposed action have not been carefully or exhaustively investigated. EIA systems have been adapted to the existing institutional context in a number of countries. Since 1985, there has been a European Community Directive on EIA (Directive 85/337).

Another tool that is becoming popular is LCA. In business and in society at large, it is increasingly understood that 'end-of-pipe' thinking in relation to environmental problems is not enough. It is also necessary to scrutinize the commodities produced by industry and to investigate each product with a 'from-cradle-to-grave' perspective. In this way, the use of natural resources and the impacts or load on the environment at each stage in the chain can be identified and assessed. A producer can then reconsider product design or put pressure on suppliers to improve their environmental performance.

A further sign of an increased emphasis on environmental performance is given by the increased popularity of voluntary EMS. Netherwood (1996, p36) defines an EMS with reference to the British Standards Institute as: 'the organizational structure, responsibilities, practices, procedures, processes and resources for determining and implementing environmental policy'.

In the same publication, Netherwood refers to Gilbert (1993) who summarized the guidelines and basic principles of environmental management, formulated by organizations such as the International Chamber of Commerce, the British Council for Sustainable Development and the Confederation of British Industry. The basic stages of an organization's EMS are described in the following terms:

- a policy statement indicating commitment to environmental improvement and conservation and protection of natural resources;
- a set of plans and programmes to implement policy within and outside the organization;
- integration of these plans into day-to-day activity and into the organizational culture;
- the measurement, audit and review of the environmental management performance of the organization against the policy, plans and programmes;
- the provision of education and training to increase understanding of environmental issues within the organization; and
- the publication of information on the environmental performance of the organization. (Gilbert, 1993, pp7–8).

There are standardized versions of EMS such as ISO 14000 and the aforementioned EMAS of 1993 according to which a specific production facility, a business corporation, or other organization can be certified or registered. We need not go into detail here about these systems, but will merely make the observation that a large number of organizations have become certified or are preparing themselves for certification by the relevant authorities.

In addition to the popularity of certification schemes, I would finally draw attention to a publication from the World Business Council for

Sustainable Development (WBCSD) with its office in Geneva. According to their own publications, 'WBCSD is a coalition of 120 international companies united by a shared commitment to the environment and to the principles of economic growth and sustainable development. Its members are drawn from 35 countries'. ABB (Asea Brown Boveri), 3M Company, The Dow Chemical Company, Du Pont, Henkel, Monsanto, Shell International Petroleum Company, Nestlé, Procter & Gamble, Danfoss and Norsk Hydro are among the members, but there are also members from other sectors, such as forestry and insurance.

In one of the more recent publications from this group *Signals for Change. Business Progress Towards Sustainable Development* the concept of 'eco-efficiency' is emphasized. It is argued that the concept makes seven main demands on companies:

1   reduce the material intensity of goods and services;
2   reduce the energy intensity of goods and services;
3   reduce toxic dispersion;
4   enhance material recyclability;
5   maximize sustainable use of renewable resources;
6   extend product durability;
7   increase the service intensity of goods and services.
(WBCSD, p10).

Although there may be some 'double talk' in these documents in the sense that the 'economic growth' and 'value added' rhetoric is still there, one can make the judgement that important developments are in train. The world view is slowly moving away from traditional monetary reductionism to a more complex idea of company activities and performance. Reference is made to the stakeholder model and to 'appropriate responsibilities of government, business and citizens' groups':

> *A growing number of business leaders realize that to achieve market success they must honor a changing array of environmental and social responsibilities.... As business people, we understand and respect the workings of the market. But we know that the market is not some ruling entity separate from human activities* (ibid, p56).

> *The media and consumers are becoming too sophisticated to allow companies to pretend; they expect real corporate action* (ibid, p51).

While all this gives some occasion for optimism, we should at the same time admit that the task ahead is no small one. Industry is largely 'locked into' its present structure and thinking habits. Inertia is part of all human structures and activities – and also of university systems, one may add. My conclusion from the above observations relates to the previous assumption that there is some heterogeneity or diversity within each actor category, for instance business leaders in large corporations, or those employed in some particular organization. For some subset of these actors or 'practical men', the perceptions and conceptual frameworks are slowly moving away from the simple world of neo-classical economics. Alternative or complementary approaches are needed to understand the arguments and ideological orientation of influential actors and the institutional changes that are taking place.

A DISAGGREGATED AND IDEOLOGICALLY OPEN CONCEPTION OF ECONOMICS

Cost–benefit analysis was described above as 'monetary reductionism' in a rather derogatory manner. What then are the alternatives? One option is to look for some other common denominator such as utilities, points or energy units, but this would only mean that one kind of reductionism is substituted for another. The alternative that will be emphasized here involves a more radical change. A holistic and disaggregated view of economics is proposed.

The use of the terms 'holistic' and 'holism' may need further clarification (cf Table 2.1). 'Holism' can be seen as being opposed to 'atomism' and holism therefore means a broadening of the scope of analysis. Analysis should not be limited to the micro-level, for instance; the broader macro-connections may well be of interest, too. Furthermore analysis can be broadened from one sector of the economy to all the sectors affected, using systems thinking. Holism can, however, also be seen as opposed to 'reductionism'. Along these lines, the reduction of complex patterns or images perceived by individuals to one-dimensional analysis can be questioned. The response to complexity suggested here is twofold:

1   a reliance on multidimensional analysis rather than one-dimensional analysis;
2   an emphasis on 'pattern thinking', 'images' and 'profiles' where numbers and calculations only represent part of the analysis.

Economics here represents the management of all kinds of resources. Non-monetary resources (natural resources, human resources, cultural resources) are thus not regarded as any 'less economic' than monetary ones. In other words, non-monetary resources are also economic, irrespective of whether we put a price tag on them or not. And whenever one refers to the monetary price of a natural resource, only the monetary aspect is thereby taken into account. Other aspects of the same resource can be described in non-monetary (but equally 'economic') terms. It is even relevant to speak of 'resource management' in situations where no money values at all are invoked in the endeavour to arrive at a wise decision.

The difference between a reductionist and a holistic view of economics is illustrated in Figure 4.1. When comparing alternative courses of action or alternative development paths, all economists would agree that there are both monetary and non-monetary impacts or indicators. As part of the reductionist view, it is argued that non-monetary impacts can be meaningfully transformed to monetary numbers (upper part of Figure 4.1), the purpose being, as we have seen, to simplify comparison between alternatives or between development paths. The monetary language is said to be well accepted in society, making the approach highly practical. Those who, like the present author, are in favour of the holistic view would say that the idea of trading one impact against another in monetary terms, while simplifying things, is at the same time dangerous. At what prices should different impacts be traded against each other? What is the price of a specific irreversible negative environmental impact, such as the (probable) loss of one species? At the societal level, prices and their interpretation are, in large measure, a matter of politics and ideology, and the role of science should therefore, it may be argued, be limited to one of elucidating an issue. Rather than the technocratic role of dictating the 'correct' prices for societal valuation, the scholar or analyst could choose a more democratic role. If reality is so complex, why should it be treated as simple? A better strategy might be to live with some degree of complexity.

While the reductionist view involves an attempt to transform all non-monetary impacts to their monetary equivalents, the holistic view means that non-monetary impacts are kept separate from monetary impacts (lower part of Figure 4.1). A disaggregated analysis is recommended where:

- impacts of various kinds (for instance different kinds of environmental impacts) are kept separate;
- spatial patterns of impact can be described;

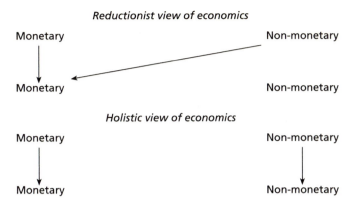

Figure 4.1 *Illustration of Reductionist and Holistic Conceptions of Economics*

- impacts on different interested parties or stakeholders can be separated;
- patterns of impact referring to different periods or points in time are kept separate.

The idea is not to maximize disaggregation, but rather to aim at a high level of disaggregation and to develop ways of visualizing the impact patterns of each alternative and especially ways of comparing the impact patterns of two alternatives considered in a decision-making situation. Among the approaches discussed earlier, EIA essentially belongs to this highly disaggregated category, although one can also find attempts to aggregate impacts as part of EIA. In the next chapter, positional analysis (PA) will be presented as an attempt to deal with both monetary and non-monetary impacts at a disaggregated level (cf Figure 4.1).

Aggregation is often (but not necessarily) less questionable at the micro level, that is for the individual household or the business corporation. It is clear that an individual living in isolation from other individuals can choose her or his own weights or prices as part of an aggregation procedure. In this case no impacts on other individuals or parties will be involved. For a household with more than one person or for a business corporation, some degree of consensus about values may similarly be assumed. But even in the case of business, the disaggregative philosophy seems to be gaining ground. Monetary calculation of investment alternatives and monetary success indicators will be important as long as present institutional arrangements prevail. Institutions change gradually, however, and one example is the growing importance of eco-efficiency indicators and environmental performance as separate efficiency categories. Monetary accounting and auditing will continue, but environmental accounting and auditing procedures are now gaining ground. Environmental management systems of the kind discussed earlier, ISO 14000 and EMAS, exemplify institutional changes that have already been introduced. Many of those actors who still limit their thinking to one-dimensionality will continue to interpret non-monetary indicators exclusively in monetary terms, though others will see the value of having two separate but complementary perspectives in which monetary evaluation is accorded the more limited role of a partial (rather than complete) analysis.

According to our premises in terms of the Political Economic Person (PEP), ethics and ideology are seen as the primary basis of valuing past, ongoing and future activities, projects or policies. 'Valuation' is then founded in the ideological orientation of individuals in specific roles and contexts. This valuation can be seen as a matching process, as previously indicated (Figure 3.2).

ANALYSIS IN TERMS OF FLOWS AND POSITIONS

As part of our holistic and disaggregated view, impacts can be categorized as in Table 4.1. In addition to the distinction between monetary and non-monetary impacts or indicators, a distinction can be made between those impacts that are expressed in terms of flows (referring to periods of time) and those that are expressed as state variables or 'positions' (referring to points in time). This will give us four categories, as indicated in Table 4.1.

Table 4.1 *Four Categories of Economic Impacts (Indicators)*

	Flow (referring to a period of time)	Position (referring to a point in time)
Monetary	I	II
Non-monetary	III	IV

The turnover of a business company and GDP at the national level exemplify monetary flow variables (category I in Table 4.1), while the assets and liabilities of a corporation at a specific point in time exemplify monetary positions (category II). On the non-monetary side, the annual outflow of cadmium pollution from a factory exemplifies a flow (category III) and the content of cadmium in the soil at a specific place and point in time represents a position (category IV). The number of species of a particular kind in a forest ecosystem is another example of a non-monetary position. All kinds of impacts are potentially relevant and analyses of monetary flows will be helpful in understanding changes in monetary positions. Similarly, non-monetary flows can certainly help in explaining what happens in terms of non-monetary positions. If one has to economize in measurement on the non-monetary side, measurement in terms of positions is often a good idea. A series of non-monetary positions over time may be compared as a way of making judgements about whether a lake is in a healthy condition – or polluted. Such an interest in a series of non-monetary positions or states is radically different from the discounting procedure and 'present values' of CBA, where it is assumed that future impacts can somehow be compressed to a single point in time.

Let us look at one activity or a set of activities in one specific organization. In our example, the organization is a farm and our farmer is growing wheat on a specific field. For this purpose the farmer uses a number of inputs, for instance nitrogen fertilizer, chemical pesticides, fuel for his farm machines, his own labour in terms of hours and a specific number of acres of open land.

How do we measure efficiency and performance in this case? According to the holistic and disaggregated view, a distinction should be made between monetary and non-monetary efficiency and performance. On the monetary side, the farmer may carry out a cost–revenue analysis (CRA), with the costs including purchases of fertilizers, pesticides and fuel, while for selling his wheat at a set price, the farmer receives a certain revenue. Costs and revenues are monetary flows, that is they refer to a period of time, for instance between t_0 and t_1, and it is possible to measure the farmer's profits, or perhaps we should say his contribution to covering fixed costs (loans for farm buildings, etc). As a result of his activities in the period, there will be not only monetary flows of the kind indicated but, connected with these flows, changes in monetary positions. I mentioned earlier that monetary positions can be described in balance sheets (with separate figures for assets and liabilities of various kinds) for the beginning and end of a period, for instance a calendar year. As a result of producing and marketing wheat (and other activities on the farm), the monetary position (balance sheet) may be improved or impaired between the beginning and the end of the year.

The monetary analysis indicated is one-dimensional, but it is not necessarily a simple one. More than one monetary efficiency or performance indicator may be needed to get a good picture of what transpired during the year. The monetary performance of two periods can be compared with reference to Figure 4.2. Profit, (or some other similar indicator) may increase or decrease when period t_1–t_2 is compared with t_0–t_1. Depending on the monetary flows during the

Position	Inflow	Activity	Outflow	Position

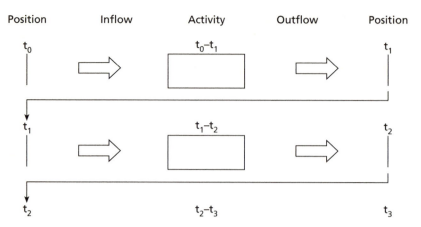

Figure 4.2 *Frame of Reference for a Discussion of Performance and Efficiency in Monetary and Non-Monetary Terms*

two periods, there will be changes in monetary positions from point in time t_0 to t_1 and from t_1 to t_2. The monetary position at t_2 can, furthermore, be compared with that at t_0.

It is argued here that some part of this philosophy of reasoning and analysis in terms of monetary flows and positions can be carried over to the non-monetary side. However, a large number of non-monetary dimensions are normally relevant rather than just one and this increases the complexity of non-monetary analysis to some extent. Returning now to the case of our farmer, quantities of material inputs into wheat production (fertilizers, pesticides, fuel) can be measured for the period considered. The yield of wheat can be related to the number of acres on the input side in an attempt to get an idea of productivity or efficiency. But there are other, less desirable outflows, for instance the leaching of nitrogen and pesticides to nearby water courses and lakes. Not only surface waters but groundwater can also be deleteriously affected by agriculture.

It is very common to focus on productivity in the sense of a ratio between a desired output (wheat) and some quantified input (that is connected with a significant portion of monetary costs) such as hours of labour or acres of land. Success stories can then be told about efficiency improvements, for instance increases in wheat yield per acre (or milk yield per cow) by 5 per cent from one year to the next. The picture may change however if one, in addition, relates wheat production to quantities of fertilizer applied on the field. From this one learns that a number of ratios between outflows and inflows can provide a broader picture of the activity or production process under consideration. With three kinds of relevant inputs and three kinds of quantifiable outputs, one gets nine ratios. Even more ratios can be constructed by relating desirable outflow (wheat) to undesirable outflow (nitrogen leaching) from the field.

What happens in flow terms will influence changes in terms of states or positions. A number of variables may be relevant to describe positions in relation to some particular agricultural activity. In our case, various indicators may be used to study the state or position of the soil, the state of nearby groundwater and surface water, nearby ecosystems whose biodiversity may be affected by the use of pesticides, and so on. Even the health of members of the farmer's family or their social position may be regarded as a relevant parameter. What will happen between t_0 and t_1 in these positional terms? Will there be an improvement or deterioration in all respects, or some mixture of both?

In addition to measuring changes in ratio (productivity) between two periods, it becomes relevant to focus on how the position changes from t_0 to t_1 and from t_1 to t_2 or when one compares t_0 with t_2, etc. As already indicated, measurement in terms of non-monetary positions is often a good idea. A series of non-monetary positions over time (for instance concerning the state of groundwater with respect to specific pollutants) may be compared as a way of making judgements about whether groundwater (or the soil in a particular area) is in a healthy condition.

From all this it can be concluded that it is not enough to study monetary flows as in CRA (at the level of the organization) or in CBA (at the societal level). In addition, monetary positions are of interest. But, again, monetary analysis is only partial analysis. It is often a good idea to identify non-monetary flows and positional changes as well. This can be the starting point for accounting, control and management of various processes or activities and be done for various subfields, such as human health, social aspects, ecosystem health and other dimensions related to natural resources and the environment.

While we have chosen specific agricultural activities as our example, it is clear that the same conceptual frame of reference can be applied to activities at the level of the individual, the private household, the business corporation or a public institution such as a university, a library or a hospital. In relation to environmental problems, it is of interest not only to study the same activity in the same organization over time. The 'cradle-to-grave' idea suggests that it is also valuable to link the activity discussed in Figure 4.2 to activities where inputs (fertilizers and pesticides) are being produced. As part of these more horizontal linkages (in the terms suggested by Figure 4.2), it is also of interest to study what happens to the wheat during later stages of the cycle (transportation, storage, milling, refining, food production, waste disposal and so on).

CONCLUSIONS ON EFFICIENCY, RATIONALITY AND IDEOLOGY

Our political economics approach emphasizes that there are many ideologies and ideological orientations in society, rather than one. In a democracy, such differences in ideologies and ideological orientations, as well as tensions between advocates of the different ideologies, are seen as normal and, with some exceptions, respected.

The neo-classical idea of pointing out one specific ideology as the only one which is 'correct', 'rational' and 'efficient' for the purposes of resource allocation does not sit well with our ideas about a normally functioning democracy. In a democracy, each person is, in principle, encouraged to form her or his specific ideological orientation and look for other individuals who more or less share this view.

According to our reasoning, there are as many ideas about rationality and efficiency as there are ideologies and ideological orientations represented in society. CBA is based on the unrealistic assumption that all citizens, for example in Sweden, share the specific market ideology built into the approach. A more fruitful idea is to regard valuation, rationality and efficiency as based on an actor's ideological orientation, or an interpretation of the ideological orientation of a group, such as a political party. Since the analyst preparing a study as part of a democratic decision-making process cannot make one analysis of efficient resource allocation for each ideological orientation represented among politicians and citizens, some more practical approach is needed. The best she or he can do appears to be to carry out a many-sided analysis of alternatives and impacts and try to articulate a limited number of possibly relevant competing ideological orientations. On the basis of this, conditional conclusions can be drawn, that is conclusions that are conditional in relation to each ideological orientation articulated and considered. The idea is to facilitate learning processes and decision-making and not to dictate the 'correct' way of arriving at the best and optimal decision. This is in fact one of the ideas underlying the approach to be described in the next chapter.

Chapter 5

Political Ideologies, Democracy and Decision-Making

If rationality and efficiency are related to ideology and ideological orientation, then our next task is to discuss possible ideological orientations. There are orientations which have influenced political developments over a period of time and have become established political ideologies, such as liberalism, conservatism and reformistic socialism. There are other '-isms' which are newer but are beginning to grow in importance in many parts of the world, for instance in Sweden or mainland Europe. Textbooks on political ideologies nowadays also include 'ecologism' and 'feminism' (Eccleshall et al, 1994; Larsson, 1994). Even 'islamism' is discussed as a political ideology (Larsson, 1997, pp149–56).

Since political ideologies are highly relevant as part of our 'political economics approach', we shall say a few words about liberalism and ecologism. How do these ideologies deal with problems related to the environment and development? Does a specific ideology offer a fruitful means–ends philosophy and environmental strategy, or does it rather assume that environmental problems are of secondary importance, that they do not exist, or perhaps that they do exist but are easy to deal with?

As indicated several times in this book, some of the ideas that play a significant role in political debate stem from economists. What is referred to as 'neo-liberalism' is a good example and was inspired by economists like Milton Friedman and political devotees, such as Prime Minister Margaret Thatcher of Great Britain. The word 'thatcherism' has been coined to denote an extreme reliance on a market ideology, that is seeing the market as the sole basis for resource allocation. According to this view, the role of national governments should be minimized, while 'deregulation' and 'privatization' are encouraged and are expected to be beneficial in almost all cases. Other -isms which point in a similar direction of market hegemony are 'consumerism' and 'economism', terms that have mostly been used in a pejorative sense.

Neo-classical economics is a specific means–ends philosophy and can, as we have seen, be interpreted in ideological terms. It places a strong emphasis on the market as the solution to all kinds of problems with specific recommendations about how to regard and think about markets. When markets do not exist, reference is made to 'shadow markets' or 'hypothetical markets'. The idea of rationality and 'efficient resource allocation' is connected with cost–benefit analysis (CBA), that is a specific market ideology.

How and where do the advocates of all these different ideologies meet? What are the rules of the game when liberals discuss environmental problems with reform socialists or ecologists? Do they fight each other using all possible means, or are they able to listen to and learn from each other? 'Democracy' is put forward here as a 'meta-ideology', as an ideology that is the subject of consensus among the majority of the political parties existing in our part of the world. We should therefore discuss the meaning of democracy.

If democracy is accepted as a meta-ideology that establishes the 'rules of the game' for political action and interaction, then the next question becomes one of clarifying the demands on decision processes to make them compatible with democracy. Although there is a generally high degree of consensus about the meaning of democracy in most respects, there are also some differences that deserve attention. Returning once more to CBA as our example, this approach is built on a specific idea of democracy which, as I see it, does not go well with what I understand as being the dominant, more egalitarian, idea of democracy.

LIBERALISM AND ITS RELATIONSHIP TO ECONOMICS

It has previously been argued that it is not realistic for an economist to claim value neutrality. To claim value neutrality while writing about political ideologies is perhaps even less reasonable. Some degree of honesty and openness with respect to one's own values and an ambition to illuminate an issue from many angles are more appropriate aspirations.

Liberalism focuses very much on the individual and her or his capacity for self-fulfilment. A 'minimal state' is sometimes advocated – which makes critics speak of 'asocial liberalism' – but the more common tendency is to point in the direction of a 'social liberalism', relegating the role of the state to one of promoting a degree of equality and social security.

Liberalism is built on a set of fundamental political rights and freedoms: freedom of speech, freedom of religion and freedom of organization as well as the right (and even encouragement) to vote and otherwise express one's political opinion are examples of this. Furthermore, liberals are reformists who believe in representative democracy. Political debate is seen as a form of learning by interaction and a way of arriving at well-informed decisions.

When it comes to organizing the economy, liberals are in favour of private property. More socially inclined liberals are ready to attribute some role of ownership and control to the population at large, represented by 'state' and 'municipalities', and therefore advocate a mixed economy (as opposed to an extreme market economy on the one hand and a socialist state economy on the other). John Maynard Keynes (1883–1948), the renowned economist, was also a member of the Liberal Party in Britain. He was among those who in the 1930s advocated a mixed economy 'in which the state assumes overall management of investment and consumption, while leaving production in the hands of private enterprise' (Eccleshall, 1994, p54). In the same period, the so-called Stockholm School of Economics, with Bertil Ohlin as one of the more prominent members, was active and held similar views. Ohlin later became the leader of the Liberal Party (Folkpartiet) in Sweden.

There are other individuals who have combined the roles of economist and political philosopher. John Stuart Mill (1806–1873) is an early example. He is known not only for his *Principles of Political Economy* (1848), but also for On Liberty which he wrote in 1859. And today, if one looks around departments of economics in Europe or the US, it is not difficult to find professors who believe in, and through their teaching actively support, a liberal market ideology.

When compared with other ideologies, liberalism appears to have a strength both historically and in contemporary political affairs in its emphasis on political rights and freedoms as well as on representative democracy. At the same time, many liberals appear to have a penchant for extreme forms of 'market liberalism' and the accumulation of private wealth. Market liberalism can be described as 'economic freedom' in the sense of a free trade of goods and services, and the unrestricted movement of capital and labour within and between countries. The previous EEC and the present EU is based on the 'four freedoms' mentioned.

The ideology of the dominant neo-classical theory in economics is very similar to, if not equivalent to, market liberalism. Neo-classical economics therefore tends to legitimize market liberalism with its focus on private property and markets for capital, labour and commodities, and with 'profits' and 'economic growth' as its main aspirations. 'Market liberalism' is not only the ideological message we hear from the majority of our politicians, but also from a majority of professors in economics. If we consider departments of economics in Sweden, it is true that one can find a number of professors with a leaning toward the Social Democratic Party. While lecturing and conducting research essentially as part of the neo-classical paradigm, they may be aware of the ideological issues involved. Villy Bergström, a former colleague of mine at the Department of Economics, Uppsala University, now with the Bank of Sweden, somewhat submissively commented on this by saying that 'taking a doctorate in economics is equal to taking a doctorate in liberalism'.

It would be unfair to say that liberals do not recognize the existence of environmental problems. Liberals as well as many neo-classical economists (with their liberal orientation) are aware of these problems. Neo-classical economists have even developed 'neo-classical environmental economics' as a specific branch or extension of their paradigm. But I feel it is fair to argue that liberals and neo-classical economists see environmental problems as being of secondary importance or being relatively easy to deal with within the scope of their ideology and paradigm.

Politicians with a liberal orientation continue to see the market and economic growth as the solution to all problems, while neo-classical economists, who also believe in markets, suggest at best a modification of existing markets in the sense that environmental costs to third parties should be internalized according to the 'polluter pays' principle. Sometimes one also sees proposals to add some new, institutionally designed markets, for instance 'bubble markets'. There are cases where environmental charges have been implemented and thereby have reduced environmental problems. But this readiness in theory to correct the market for externalities appears too seldom to be reflected in policy and practice. One possible reason, that was hinted at earlier (Chapter 2), is that proposals to correct the market contradict and infringe on the idea of perfectly functioning markets. Liberal politicians and economists alike may also realize that a systematic correcting of prices for environmental impacts of all kinds of commodities will actually take us several steps away from the market economy and instead closer to a planned economy. And such a development is inconceivable for liberals as well as neo-classicists.

ECOLOGISM AND ITS RELATIONSHIP TO ECONOMICS

While market liberals get plenty of conceptual and ideological support at departments of economics, attitudes to those who believe in 'ecologism' of one kind or another are rather different. Although things may be improving slightly as we approach the end of the 1990s, the best judgement I can make is that those who take environmental problems seriously will be met with indifference, if not hostility, in these departments. This can be explained in part by the fact that 'ecologism' as an ideology is not yet well established. Another explanation is, however, that this means–ends philosophy does not fit well with the ideology of neo-classical economics.

In a textbook on political ideologies, Michael Kenny first notes that the present environmental crisis has led to ideological debate in many circles and that a large number of distinctions have been made, for instance between 'environmentalists' and 'conservationists', 'light Greens' and 'dark Greens' and between 'light ecologists' and 'dark ecologists' (Kenny, 1994, p219). At the same time, Kenny cautions us about these dualisms which may be too simplistic to capture the complexity of the current ideological debate in Europe and elsewhere.

One distinction that Kenny – as well as another commentator in this debate, Andrew Dobson (1995) – finds meaningful is the one between 'environmentalism' and 'ecologism'. 'Environmentalism', according to Kenny, involves an attempt 'to deploy the techniques and ideas of the mainstream to achieve a cleaner and environmentally safer version of contemporary society' (Kenny, 1994, p219) 'Environmentalism' does not really challenge 'the competitive and individualistic ethos' of our societies or the 'commitment to economic growth' (ibid, p220). It is believed that we can carry on as before with some modified version of market liberalism where, for instance, gross domestic product (GDP) as an indicator of success is modified to a 'Green GDP', that is yet another monetary indicator. 'Ecologism', on the other hand, is more of a challenge to mainstream thinking and ideology. While building on present society and its historical background, it involves a readiness to reconsider the development path and institutional arrangements of our society. New visions are needed in addition to those connected with industrialism and capitalism. Neither state capitalism as in the former USSR, nor private or market capitalism as in the present EU or the USA, represents the final answer.

All this has to begin with new thinking and 'ideological debate'. And in this case, the recommendation to engage in ideological debate does not mean that somebody possesses the 'correct' answer to the ideological challenges faced. In general terms, however, it can be stated that even paradigms and thinking in economics need to be involved. Neo-classical economics and neo-classical 'environmental economics' can be connected with 'environmentalism' in the above sense, while 'ecological economics' is closer to 'ecologism'. If one prefers, reference can be made to an 'economics of environmentalism' and an 'economics of ecologism', respectively.

But let us return to Kenny's textbook on political ideologies. He identifies a number of recurrent themes as part of 'ecologism' (ibid, pp230–7), which will be elaborated on here and modified somewhat.

Sustainability

A first theme in 'ecologism' is an idea not to degrade the human environment and its ecosystems and natural resources. In addition to ecological sustainability, social sustainability (or rather socio-cultural sustainability) is an important imperative. Just as ecological diversity is seen as a good thing, the same tends to be true of cultural diversity in the sense that local cultures with their traditions, customs and wealth of knowledge tend to be seen both as values in themselves and as an important resource.

Population and the Load on the Environment

Human beings compete for space, both with each other and with non-human forms of life. Agricultural land is needed for food production and the inhabitants of one country can utilize and exploit agricultural land in other countries through international trade. Reference is often made to 'environmental space' or an 'ecological footprint' in the sense that the inhabitants of a specific municipality, region or country need a specific amount of space for food production or waste assimilation, which may be much bigger than the municipality, region or country itself. Agricultural production in The Netherlands, for example, requires considerable arable land in Thailand for fodder production. Another part of the load on the environment, which may threaten ecosystem services in the long run and outcompete other life forms, is pollution from human activities. The ozone layer and climatic change (global warming) are two examples, but there are many forms of chemical pollution that represent problems in this sense.

Each individual with a particular ideological orientation and consequent life-style 'consumes' a certain quantity of natural resources and contributes with pollution to a certain extent. For each region or country, estimates of average per capita load on the environment can be made for specific parameters. Such estimates suggest that the lifestyle in the Western countries at the end of the 20th century (which is held as the ideal by many other countries) is not sustainable. Increases in population density, whether regionally or on a global level, exacerbate the problem and it is clear that continued, uninhibited human expansion will force aside, or otherwise affect, other forms of life.

Organizational and Institutional Frameworks

A third theme relates to the way society and economy are organized. Advocates of ecologism often point to the virtues of smaller, more decentralized human communities. Friedrich Schumacher's book *Small is Beautiful* (1973) proposes a move in the direction of 'human-scale' dimensions as opposed to the tendencies to praise 'big business' and large-scale technology. Largely 'self-governing' communities are suggested, as opposed to the 20th century tendencies towards 'economic integration' with respect to goods, services, capital and labour. Internationalization and 'globalization' may have their advantages, but they also encompass a number of threats. Rather than arguing in favour of free trade and international integration in every respect, the ecologist may maintain that promotion of the population's health, protection of the environment, protection of a local culture with its language, customs, values and knowledge, can be more important. Pollution from transportation of goods over large distances is a major threat to people and ecosystems on a regional and global level. Transnational business with the whole world as its 'hunting-ground' can be questioned. The previous General Agreement on Tariffs and Trade (GATT) and the present World Trade Organization (WTO) tend to facilitate global penetration for international business in a way which (hopefully) may make international business leaders themselves wonder about their increasing power and responsibility.

A spiritual and an Ethical Dimension

A fourth theme concerns a transformation of 'consciousness' about our relationships with nature and ecosystems. Gradually modifying our present economies and social arrangements to achieve a more sustainable society will release all kinds of human potential, the 'spiritual' aspects included. It has been argued that economists are the 'high priests' of our time and their text and message, as spelled out in neo-classical microeconomics textbooks, has not been above promoting a tendency to worship material goods, money and 'the market' (Henderson, 1981). 'Marketing' efforts and the enthusiasm presented in textbooks by Philip Kotler (1997) and others in business management education are entirely consistent with the present course of the market economy, but unfortunately are not compatible with attempts to change life-styles to make them more conducive to sustainable development.

The market economy liberates the market actor from social constraints, which may be advantageous in many situations, though that which is 'freedom' for one actor may limit the freedom of other actors or collectives of individuals at all levels, the global level included. Freedom should therefore entail responsibility. But the business corporation, for example, is in many ways an organization having 'limited responsibility'. Similarly, neo-classical consumer theory tends to be silent about ethics and about the responsibility of the consumer. Advocates of 'ecologism' would argue that individual responsibility is an important element of a sustainable society and that contemporary political economic systems have too often tended to remove responsibility from the individual. This is true not only of state capitalism, or Social Democracy in the Swedish version, but also of most market economies. In what way can one make actors in the market economy more responsible for the environmental, health-related and cultural aspects of their behaviour?

Science and Technology

Science and technology have long been regarded as the key to progress. In his book *Development Betrayed*, Richard Norgaard speaks about the 'illusions of progress' and also maintains a more divided view of the role of science and technology (Norgaard, 1994). In Table 2.1, traditional 'Western' scientific premises such as objectivity and value neutrality were presented together with more recent epistemological principles that are gaining support. At the end of the 1990s, one could question the claims of value neutrality as being a form of 'institutionalized social irresponsibility' (just as joint stock companies are characterized by specific forms of limited responsibility). It is certainly a comfortable attitude. While keeping many interpretations alive, one should not readily dismiss the possibility that the ideas of 'objectivity' and 'value neutrality' have been 'socially constructed' by scientists to serve specific purposes, for instance safeguarding their prestige and power. The scientists can then claim they are innocent when 'scientific knowledge' is applied in society and things go wrong.

Technology has similarly been associated with optimism. Many actors – even some who regard themselves as environmentalists – still seem to believe that almost all environmental problems can be 'solved' with the help of new technology. Just as is the case of markets, a conditional view about scientific and technological research and its consequences is recommended. The results depend largely upon the values and attitudes of researchers and engineers. Where economics as a 'science' and even 'technology' (referring to various methods or 'tools') is concerned, there is further reason to engage in new, critical thinking. Attempts to reconsider conceptual frameworks, visions and theories as parts of a pluralistic attitude are to be encouraged.

The conditional view of markets, science and technology suggested is based on an assumption that there is a heterogeneity or diversity within each actor category such as market actors, scientists, engineers and even economists. There are certainly some who have internalized very little in the way of environmental concerns, but there exist also actors, networks of actors and collectives who have emphasized environmental considerations in their activities. Just as market liberalism has long been applauded among university scholars, engineers and businessmen, the role of 'ecologism', or a new combination of ecologism and liberalism, may hopefully be increasing in many circles – universities and transnational corporations not excluded.

Transition to a 'Green' Society

Any transformation of our present political–economic system has to start with the individual and her or his visions of a different society. This transformation requires ideological debate and debate about paradigms in economics, both of which are important. The individual acts in a specific socio-institutional context, where rules connected with democracy are an important part.

It can be argued that the strength of our present political–economic system lies in our reliance on democracy rather than in the role of markets. As regards organizations and markets, major reforms appear to be necessary, though it may prove difficult to find ways and means to accomplish this. For example, energy use in the transportation of goods and people has to be reduced significantly and the establishment of local businesses and markets encouraged. The ongoing transfer of power from local municipalities and national governments to supranational bodies like the EU and transnational corporations does not seem to solve many environmental problems. Taxation policies could play an important role as part of a transition to a greener society. Further internationalization of stock markets and other capital flows does not appear to be in the interest of global stability, but leads rather to its opposite, global vulnerability as indicated by events in south-east Asia in the mid-1990s.

It appears to be necessary to counteract some of the present development trends which are pursued largely by transnational corporations and other financial interests. Corporate leaders are often in a position where they can threaten particular workers, local municipalities or even countries, by pointing out lower wages and otherwise 'better' conditions for production in some other municipality or country. So called 'outsourcing' is legitimized by reference to 'competitive pressure', a 'need for increased efficiency' and 'necessary structural change'. In the short run, this strategy involves 'winners' as well as 'losers' when judged in terms of traditional monetary ideas of efficiency. Since structural change will continue, no municipality can feel secure and in the long run all municipalities and countries may well lose out as a result of this very 'dynamic' system.

DEMOCRACY AS A META-IDEOLOGY

Democracy can be described as a means–ends philosophy and in that sense it qualifies as an 'ideology'. It is a specific kind of ideology, however, which does not so much refer to the substance of policies and politics, but rather to the rules of the game when policy is formed and decisions are taken. It is a form of government which accepts or encourages a large number of power centres and a plurality of competing perspectives and opinions. Democracy can also be defined by reference to its opposite which is a far-reaching concentration of power; in the extreme case, political dictatorship.

In terms of social change and decision processes, our main concern, democracy, is related to the fundamental human rights previously listed as part of liberalism, namely freedom of speech, freedom of religion and the right to organize for political and other purposes. Democracy stands for the ambition to empower the people and this is, in part, connected with the right to vote in political elections. That each person has one vote suggests equality of opportunities to influence social and political affairs, at least in this respect. But our ideas about democracy should not be limited to the ballot. There are other dimensions of 'participation' in political life.

In discussing democracy, one sometimes gets the impression that everything is possible in terms of influencing social change or a specific decision process. An actor who tries to influence the development of a particular issue will, however, meet a number of other actors and interested parties with different ideological orientations and commitments in relation to the issue under consideration. Our actor will meet not only enthusiasm and open doors but also barriers and even locked doors. In a metaphorical sense, democracy can be seen as an attempt to increase the relative number of open doors.

One of my first attempts to influence a decision process at the municipal level was through a newspaper article in *Upsala Nya Tidning* in 1971 about a planned multi-storey car park in the town centre. At that time, there was a tendency to 'solve' transportation problems by planning and building new car parks. In the case of a first car park, the planning process was more or less completed. Six months later a second car park, 'Draken', even closer to a pedestrian precinct in the city centre, was mooted. I wrote a second article questioning whether this was a sensible way to deal with transportation and environmental issues, even from the point of view of the shopping centres being situated close to the planned car park. I also expressed my belief that influential politicians and other actors were already committed to this specific solution and that it was, therefore, probably meaningless to suggest other ways of dealing with the issue. Contrary to my expectations, a leading politician responded in the newspaper, saying that it was still possible to reconsider plans for this area. This was actually done and a compromise reached, and only underground parking space was permitted.

A planning and decision process, such as this one, can be seen as a series of opening and closing of doors. In terms of tendencies to close doors rather than to open them, we can speak of the following kinds of commitment:

- cognitive commitments;
- emotional commitments;
- social commitments;
- political commitments;
- market oriented commitments;
- action oriented commitments;
- legal commitments;
- physical commitments.

Different networks and groups may work towards different solutions to a planning issue and for one group the process may start with the ideas or visions of a single actor (commitment in a cognitive and emotional dimension), which are communicated to other actors and interested parties (commitments in social and possibly political and market dimensions), which then may lead to a commitment within a political party or coalition of political parties. This in turn may pave the way for a formal proposal to build according to plan. The plan may be made known to the public and all interested parties via a presentation or an exhibition. Some of the comments received as part of this process normally lead to a modification of the initial plan and at some stage a decision is taken by the municipal political assembly (a political and legal commitment) which in turn leads to the commencement of construction activities (a change in the physical dimensions). In an attempt to make sense of processes of this kind, I have referred to various sorts of inertia and a principle of successive commitments (Söderbaum, 1973). In its initial stages the process can be quite open and the imperatives of democracy tell us that attempts to close the process at an early stage for the benefit of specific market actors, or other interested parties, should be counteracted.

The whole issue of democracy in relation to planning and decision processes should be seen in this light. In addition to intellectual and knowledge-related activities, a power game is taking place with a number of actors and interested parties involved. These actors and parties appear on the scene with all their vested interests and habitual thinking patterns. In relation to this, 'democracy' can be seen as an attempt to counterbalance the influence of those who, by controlling property and in other ways, are more powerful than others.

The principles of democracy state that all stakeholders or interested parties should be encouraged to 'participate' in the planning and decision process. Participation thus refers to the right to be informed about what is going on. Each party should be respected and should be able to influence the process. A willingness to listen and learn should characterize all actors and interested parties. Ideally, each actor should be open to the possible value of the ideological thinking and orientations of others and to their ideas about theories and methods. There should be a search for consensus, but also a readiness to accept and understand that the actors and interested parties do not share the same vision, and that a conflict of interest is a normal state of affairs. Such conflicting views should be dealt with as constructively as possible and indeed represent a source of creativity and new thinking for all actors and stakeholders.

Arenas should be institutionally designed so that actors and interested parties can meet in open dialogue. The rules of the game should be such that understanding and trust has a good prospect of being developed, as opposed to misunderstanding and mistrust. For this reason the planning and decision process should be as transparent as possible. The actions of specific actors should be visible, thereby encouraging responsible behaviour and making social control possible. The process should be documented with the aid of protocols and in other ways.

Analysis of competing alternatives should be 'many-sided' and thereby encourage new thinking. The analyst should counteract any tendency of specific stakeholder groups or networks to reduce the number of alternatives, the kinds of impacts or valuational viewpoints considered. Some methods will work to strengthen democracy in this respect, while other approaches may increase misunderstandings and conflict in society.

Finally, when a decision has been taken through the usual process of majority voting, it should be possible to follow up the behaviour of various actors/interested parties in order to learn from past successes and failures. Open criticism of what is perceived as 'manipulation' of the planning and decision process should be possible, as well as lawsuits in cases where one party believes that another stakeholder has contravened the law in some respect.

A CLASSIFICATION OF APPROACHES TO DECISION-MAKING

The previous 'imperatives of democracy' point in a specific direction concerning approaches to decision-making at a societal level. The same imperatives can also be applied to the issue of democracy in business and other organizations.

Approaches to decision-making can be classified as belonging either to a 'highly aggregated' category or a 'highly disaggregated' category. CBA belongs to the former category. An attempt is made to measure all 'costs' and 'benefits' for all affected parties and all time periods that are considered relevant, in monetary terms, and add them to a present value. Positional analysis (PA), which is presented here as an alternative approach, is a highly disaggregated approach in the sense that impacts of different kinds and concerning different interested parties and different time periods are kept separate throughout the analysis. This analysis is built on an alternative idea of rationality, where the ideological orientation of each actor or decision maker is matched against the expected impact profiles of each alternative considered. This is an 'adaptive' idea of rationality, rather than the one-dimensional 'optimizing' idea associated with CBA.

In addition to the degree of aggregation, another dimension becomes important when discussing various approaches or methods in relation to democracy and that is whether an approach is ethically and ideologically closed or open. Here CBA belongs to the highly ideologically closed category and builds upon a specific market ideology, where the analyst refers to specific methods of identifying the 'correct prices' of various impacts for the purposes of resource allocation, while PA is more open-ended. PA results in conditional conclusions related to ideological orientations that are possibly relevant for specific decision makers.

This means that we have four categories of approach to decision-making, as shown in Table 5.1. CBA belongs to category I, and PA to category IV. Among the highly aggregated approaches, there are alternatives to CBA. Rather than using money as the common denominator, one can, for instance, refer to points and a system of weighting. I know of a case from the late 1970s, for instance, where three options for the construction of a road between two geographical points were considered. The alternatives were compared along three dimensions: trafficability (ie time saving compared with the existing road), safety (ie an ambition to minimize risks of various kinds), and an 'aesthetic' dimension (which in this case referred to views of the landscape from the vehicle driver's position, and possibly also to environmental impacts). Each alternative was given 1 to 5 points for each of the three dimensions (trafficability, safety, aesthetics). In the version of this exercise that I happened to see, different weights were also assigned to each dimension. Trafficability was weighted 5, safety 4 and aesthetics 1. The alternative which would give the quickest passage between the two geographical points received 5 points for trafficability which was then multiplied by the weighting 5; 4 points for security which was multiplied by 4; and 2 points for aesthetics which was multiplied by 1. The sum of this aggregation is 43 points. A similar operation is undertaken for each of the other two alternatives to find the alternative with the highest scores.

Table 5.1 *A Classification of Approaches to Decision-Making*

	Ideologically closed	Ideologically open
Highly aggregated	I	II
Highly disaggregated	III	IV

We will now discuss the difference between CBA and the multi-criteria approaches. Both approaches build on the idea of aggregation, but it is clear that the multi-criteria approach does not claim to supply the sole correct solution. The approach is instead used to clarify a dialogue between actors (cf category II). As distinguished from CBA, the multi-criteria approach is transparent from the point of view of all actors and interested parties. While actor A may have suggested the dimensions of comparison shown, as well as the impact estimates and weights, actor B may have a different opinion in all three respects. B may suggest that A has omitted what she or he sees as important impacts, that other weights are more in line with B's thinking and values, and so on.

It is also possible to conceive of an approach based on the adaptive idea of rationality, but which is ideologically closed (cf category III). At the micro-level, one individual may have to decide for her- or himself which commodities to buy or which activities to engage in, and in such a case it may be less relevant to bring in the opinions and values of others.

As was discussed in relation to Figure 4.1, Environmental Impact Assessment (EIA) is a more or less institutionalized approach in a number of countries. While most varieties of EIA belong to category IV, one can also find examples of attempts to aggregate different kinds of environmental impacts. It should furthermore be made clear that the distinction between only two categories along each dimension in Table 5.1 represents a simplification. Even intermediate categories may be relevant, for instance in terms of aggregation. So-called cost-effectiveness analysis, for instance, is less aggregated than CBA, since it is two-dimensional rather than one-dimensional, the monetary cost of achieving a specific non-monetary (environmental) objective being minimized. In terms of an ideology being closed, the approach is comparable to CBA.

CBA, PA and EIA are all approaches designed mainly for use at the societal level. The imperatives of democracy may be relevant, however, even for business corporations and other organizations. For this and other reasons, disaggregated approaches can also be useful at the level of organizations.

DEMOCRACY AND DECISION-MAKING

A compatibility test can now be applied at the level of specific methods. Is CBA compatible with our imperatives of democracy? Is PA compatible with the same imperatives?

For each of the two approaches or methods, the following questions can be asked:

- Does the approach systematically compare alternatives on equal terms, ie without prejudice as to the best option?
- Does the approach dictate the ethical or valuational standpoint to be applied, or leave them open to debate and independent judgement by decision makers?
- Does the approach encourage dialogue and a mutual learning process with all of the stakeholders and actors involved?

- Is the approach comprehensible for stakeholders and interested parties? Will they be able to perceive in what way their interests have been considered? Is the process transparent?
- Does the approach lead to a reasonable allocation of roles between analyst, politician, stakeholder and other citizens? Does it encourage responsible behaviour by different actors and/or stakeholders? Will, for instance, the method make each decision maker responsible for her or his decisions or will there rather be a tendency to shift responsibility to the analyst and the method used?

In my judgement, it is only according to the first criterion that CBA is compatible with our imperatives of democracy. CBA represents an attempt to give each alternative an equal chance as part of a systematic comparison. Unfortunately, CBA is a biased approach in other respects. As has been argued before, CBA is closed in ideological terms and reflects a specific market ideology among all possible market ideologies and other ideologies. For example, CBA is very different from, and incompatible with, the ideology of 'ecologism' as previously described in this chapter. CBA is also a technocratic approach, where the CBA analyst is seen as an expert in an extreme sense, that is someone who need not engage in a dialogue with other stakeholders. The analyst only observes actual market prices and market behaviour.

Although CBA may appear simple and straightforward with its focus on money, some stakeholders and other actors may experience difficulties in reconciling their own perceptions of the issue faced (for instance a road planning issue) and the simplistic analysis offered as part of CBA. Since everything is traded in money terms, non-monetary impacts as well as conflicts of interest will fade away. In real life, most people understand that one has to live with some part of these complexities.

When it comes to the allocation of roles, the use of CBA can be seen as an attempt to render politicians unnecessary (cf Table 5.2). CBA represents a specific ideology in political terms, which gets its respectability (if it has any) from economics as a science. The advocates of CBA expect us to accept this particular political ideology because it stems from a discipline that claims value-neutrality and thereby stands above or outside politics.

It is much more reasonable to argue that the CBA approach is a valuable and reasonable approach – but only for those who share the CBA ideology. If all stakeholders and citizens are considered, and not only those who share the CBA ideology, it becomes clear that the CBA approach can no longer be considered acceptable in a democratic society. It is this ideological dictatorship by CBA advocates and neo-classical economists more generally, which has made some commentators speak of 'technocracy' (Fischer, 1990) or 'econocracy' (Self, 1975). My conclusion, therefore, is that CBA is at best compatible with a specific kind of 'market democracy', one where money is the basis of voting power as part of 'willingness to pay' approaches, etc. As we all know, the potential or capacity to vote in monetary terms and thereby influence an issue varies between individuals.

This incompatibility with democracy means that CBA should not be used at all as part of societal decision-making. CBA therefore represents one of the weaker parts of neo-classical theory and analysis. Other parts of neo-classical theory may be specific in conceptual and ideological terms, but may be defended as part of a pluralistic attitude, for example as offering insights not given by other perspectives.

When judged in relation to the criteria listed, PA, on the other hand, appears to belong to a category of approaches which are more in line with democracy. Not only are alternatives systematically compared, but the approach recognizes the existence of various ethical and ideological standpoints. PA represents an attempt to engage in a learning process with the many actors and stakeholders involved, the idea being that as many as possible should understand how their interests have been taken into consideration (or down-played) in the analysis. The role of the analyst is furthermore one of 'facilitator' in a social and political process (Table 5.2) rather than 'expert on correct values'. CBA tends to play down the issue of responsibility for decisions taken, or at best places this responsibility in the hands of those who invented the CBA approach itself or of those who more or less correctly follow its precepts. As a part of PA, each actor, whatever her or his role, is seen as responsible for her or his behaviour.

THE CONTINUED IMPORTANCE OF IDEOLOGY

It has been argued that a debate about ideology is no longer relevant. Francis Fukuyama even speaks of 'the end of history' (1989, 1992) arguing that 'liberal democracy' represents the final stage of a long history of ideological conflict between and within countries. Fukuyama and many of his friends are apparently happy with the present development trends in the USA and Europe. He has probably not understood many of the environmental and social problems in these countries and other parts of the world.

I cannot share his judgement that liberalism is unproblematic. While there is a strength in that part of liberalism which at the same time is the basis of democracy (human rights of various kinds), there is a weakness in a liberalism which preaches unrestricted 'economic

Table 5.2 *Role Attributions Connected with CBA and PA Respectively*

	CBA	PA
Analyst	'Expert' on values and CBA method	'Facilitator', expert on PA method and dialogue
Stakeholder	Essentially passive. May be asked about willingness to pay	Is encouraged to express opinions and take part in dialogue
Concerned citizen	Silence will facilitate analysis and decision process	Is encouraged to express opinions and take part in dialogue
Politician	Expected to accept the authority of analyst and the results of analysis	Decisions are based on the ideological orientation of each politician, who is thereby made responsible for her or his behaviour

freedom'. Free trade of goods and services, free movements of capital and free migration may, as we have argued before, be a threat to the health and welfare of individuals, to various cultures in different parts of the world and to the environment and natural resources. 'Protectionism' is sometimes a wise strategy, although free market enthusiasts exhibit some difficulty in understanding this. Only a liberalism which is 'liberated' from the ideological partnership with neo-classical economics may increase or regain its attractiveness.

There are many individuals who are happy to listen to Fukuyama and his storytelling or account of history. I do not exclude the possibility that his narrative is 'socially constructed' for specific ideological purposes. The argument may be grounded in certain facts, but also serves certain interests more than others. Contrary to Fukuyama, I believe that debate about the strengths and weaknesses of various ideologies is as important now as it has ever been – perhaps even more important. The international community is on the right course when new catchwords are coined, such as 'sustainable development'. This slogan may have many meanings, but its origin and use at the 1992 UN conference in Rio de Janeiro has initiated some important new thinking, not only among politicians, but in various other circles, for instance among industrialists. And this ongoing debate about sustainability and its various meanings is very much an ideological debate.

Chapter 6

Environmental Management and Decision-making: A Political Economics Approach

The forms of EMS now implemented in business and other organizations were touched upon in Chapter 4. In the present chapter, an attempt will be made to further articulate our political economics approach with the hope of throwing some light on the more standardized systems, ISO 14001 and EMAS. Environmental management will not only be discussed for business purposes, but for all kinds of organization. The conceptual framework offered claims to be useful even for households and at the level of an individual's private activities.

Neo-classical economics has little to say about the evaluation of past activities. CBA for example, is designed to deal with future oriented investment projects. It should be admitted that the more recent complementary approaches (such as EIA) and alternative approaches (such as PA) have been used mainly in connection with major investments in housing, roads, airports, energy systems and the like. But information is needed for management purposes also about past and ongoing activities. Environmental management can be oriented towards past activities, present activities or projected future activities.

Learning from history and past activities is essential for nations, municipalities, organizations and individuals alike. Present environmental performance can be compared with past environmental performance for a specific kind of activity (or for patterns of activities) and against this background objectives formulated to improve performance in the future.

Another distinction which appears in the recent debate about EMS as well as EIA is the one between:

- the impact assessment of investment projects;
- the impact assessment of programmes (comprising a number of interrelated projects);
- the impact assessment of policies.

Application of EIA has so far been mainly at the project level, while it is increasingly understood that projects are parts of 'programmes' and 'policies'. Environmental and other impacts have to be discussed at these more comprehensive levels. In the spirit of this book, our list can be continued by highlighting the need also to discuss and 'evaluate' (as we have tried to do to some extent) political ideologies and paradigms in economics with respect to environmental performance. In the present chapter, a large part of our analysis refers to ongoing activities and to project appraisal, although it is hoped that the conceptual tools offered will also be of interest in addressing policy issues (see Chapter 7).

In Chapter 5, a distinction was made between highly aggregated and highly disaggregated approaches. It was argued that the latter approaches are more compatible with democracy and in other ways are more appropriate for environmental and development issues. In this chapter, one of the disaggregated approaches, PA, will be considered in greater detail.

THE PURPOSE OF POSITIONAL ANALYSIS

PA as an approach to decision-making in business and at the societal level was first presented in a PhD thesis (Söderbaum, 1973). The 1960s and early 1970s was a period when interdisciplinary thinking became popular in different parts of the world. Cybernetics and systems theory were among the proposals discussed. In the same period, 'systems analysis' and 'policy analysis' were suggested at the more applied level. The subtitle of the aforementioned thesis was 'Economic analysis on an interdisciplinary basis'. This was also the time of the Stockholm United Nations Conference on the Human Environment (1972), when some of us felt that interdisciplinary thinking could add to our understanding of problems related to environment and development.

Mainstream neo-classical economics has been behind much of the language and conceptual framework of policy discourse and thinking about project appraisal in Sweden and since PA is not compatible with neo-classical economics, it has played only a peripheral role in relation to practical policy. On the other hand, PA and similar approaches have been in evidence in more interdisciplinary oriented fields, such as institutional economics, human ecology and also in professional fields, such as town planning and the evaluation of road and energy systems. PA has mainly been discussed and applied in the academic world. Most PA studies have been carried out in Sweden, Norway and Finland and some PhD studies can be reported.

Many scholars of my generation are content with ideas about 'expertness' inherited from the past. This platform as 'expert' is associated with power and most scholars are disinclined to listen to messages that may weaken their position. Their identity is closely connected with traditional ideas about science and they prefer to see applied studies of societal 'resource allocation' only as an extension of objective science. Myrdal's observation that 'values are always with us', is typically regarded as an attack on science itself by someone who does not understand the special role of science and technology in society.

Neo-classical economists furthermore see their science and profession as connected with mathematical, often monetary calculation. Representatives of other professions, politicians and citizens have similarly become accustomed to these ideas from economists and do not expect anything else.

When related to such habits of thought and views of the identity of economists, PA may appear to be a very strange approach. Or, to put it in the language of this book, PA is not compatible with the world view and ideological orientation of a customarily indoctrinated neo-classical economist.

The purpose of PA is one of illuminating an issue in a many-sided way with respect to:

- options or alternatives of choice;
- impacts;
- interests affected, conflicts between interests included; and
- possible ideological orientations that can be useful for valuation and decision-making.

The concept of many-sidedness means that more than one perspective can be applied (for instance in the sense that alternatives are compared systematically, not only at the level of impacts but also at the level of interests; see below). The analyst tries to do her or his best to estimate impacts in various dimensions. Both qualitative and quantitative information is used and knowledge is often fragmentary rather than complete.

The reason why a many-sided analysis is preferred has to do with the imperatives of democracy presented in Chapter 5. PA should be seen as part of a learning process for the analyst as well as for the other stakeholders and actors involved. The results of the process in the form of specific decisions and their implementation are therefore particularly dependent on the activities and knowledge of all who contribute to the process.

THE MAIN FEATURES OF PA

PA is in many ways closely connected with the conceptual framework already presented:

- *Political Economic Person (PEP) assumptions.* In management and decisionmaking processes, individuals take on different roles, for instance professional roles (stakeholder, analyst or other expert), other stakeholder (such as neighbour to a polluting factory), concerned citizen, consumer and so on. Each individual is guided by an ideological orientation, some part of which being activated in specific roles and situations.
- *Political Economic Organizations (PEO).* Just as the individual is interpreted in political terms, so is the organization as a collectivity of individuals (cf Chapter 3). Each organization is assumed to have a mission statement, which can be expressed in various non-monetary as well as monetary terms. Furthermore the organization is seen as a polycentric unit in the sense that each individual and stakeholder can potentially influence the development path of the organization. The organization is assumed to be in a position where it controls certain resources and adapts to its environment and part of this environment is, in turn, made up by various individuals and PEOs as actors.
- *Imperatives of democracy.* Management and decision-making is understood as a process involving individuals. Not only are the impacts of alternatives of choice important; so too is the decision process itself, with stakeholder participation, dialogue and co-operative learning. Do the actors and decision makers behave in a way that is compatible with democracy? Taking democracy seriously will also involve a shift in role perceptions, as suggested by Table 5.2.
- *Holistic conception of economics.* Economics and the management of resources is seen in multidimensional terms. It is assumed that resources that are non-monetary in kind have to be dealt with as such and cannot be reduced to monetary terms. Instead monetary efficiency for a specific activity has to be separated from various kinds of non-monetary efficiency, for instance 'eco-efficiency' (cf Chapter 4).
- *Conditional view of markets.* The market is seen as being neither inherently good nor inherently bad. It all depends on the rules that confront specific market actors and on their ideological orientation. Market transactions may thus lead to a degradation as well as an improvement of ecosystems and natural resources. The health

and social status or position of individuals may similarly be impaired or enhanced. Markets may be regulated by state intervention with the purpose of protecting cultural resources or the health of individuals and ecosystems, but market actors can also themselves influence the rules under which market transactions take place in a way that either impairs or improves the state of the environment and other resource positions.

- *Systems thinking.* Analysis in terms of systems can be seen as a way of transcending traditional administrative borders between disciplines, professions and sectors. No analysis can cover everything but the idea is to identify all those disciplines and professions which can contribute with knowledge when dealing with a specific issue. Similarly, all systems that are affected as part of a given decision situation can be identified as a first step in the attempt to discover the different likely impacts of the alternatives. Systems thinking also involves an awareness of systems boundaries and, in our case, an understanding of the relationships between a specific decision situation and other related, policy or decision situations.
- *Positional thinking.* The distinction between flows and positions was presented in Chapter 4. It was argued that an analysis of monetary flows and positions is seldom enough, but that a complementary analysis of non-monetary flows and positions has to be carried out. In Chapter 5, a 'principle of successive commitments' was presented as an example of 'positional thinking'. This element of PA will be further elaborated in the present chapter.
- *Analysis of activities and interests.* Dealing with environmental and development issues is very much a matter of seeking consensus about particular development paths or investment alternatives, but at the same time it is also a matter of dealing with disagreement and conflicting interests. PA rests on an assumption that it is better to make conflicting interests visible and discuss them, than to claim that an expert knows what is 'best for society'.
- *Rationality as an adaptive process.* Instead of connecting rationality with mathematical optimization, an adaptive concept of rationality is proposed. Each individual refers to her or his particular ideological orientation in valuing a particular phenomenon or alternative of choice. The task of the PA analyst is to estimate the impacts of each option considered in multidimensional or profile terms and perhaps also to suggest and articulate possible ideological orientations relevant to the decision situation. What is the meaning for instance of 'ecological sustainability' when dealing with specific transportation issues? In making her or his decision, the politician or other decision maker should, of course, refer to

her or his particular ideological orientation and test the compatibility of this orientation with the impact profiles of each alternative as part of an adaptive process (cf Figure 3.2).

- *Conditional conclusions relative to ideological orientation.* The task of the analyst may end with conditional conclusions in the sense of suggesting which alternative best matches specific ideological orientations. A neo-liberal market ideology may point to one specific alternative as being the best and a specific version of 'ecologism' may conclude that another option is preferable. Each such possible ideology should be specified with respect to attitude to risk and uncertainty. Knowledge about environmental impacts are frequently uncertain. A 'precautionary principle' will often point in a direction that differs from one based on 'technological optimism'.

Two comments will be made here on the list of the features of 'positional analysis'. First, PA is not limited to a method in a narrow sense but is based on a political economics philosophy, as has been articulated here. In this respect PA can be compared with CBA, which is based on neo-classical economics as a specific philosophy. Second, whether 'positional analysis' is an appropriate name for the approach can certainly be discussed. In some sense, all the names or terms for specific paradigms and methods have their limitations. We have become used to 'neo-classical economics' as the term for what is, so far, mainstream economics. 'Neo-classical' refers to the followers of the classical economists, but institutional economics also builds on classical economics. 'Institutional economists' certainly problematize and study 'institutions', but nowadays neo-classicists also study 'institutions', albeit in their own way. CBA is an analysis of 'costs' and 'benefits' in a specific monetary sense; PA is also an analysis of 'costs' and 'benefits', but in some broader sense.

PA borrows from systems theory to some extent (and even cybernetics where reference is sometimes made to the 'positions' of a biological unit or system) and can be described as a kind of systems analysis. The distinctiveness of PA lies, as I see it, in a specific combination of ideas and methodological elements, where 'positional thinking' is perhaps the one which best separates PA from other approaches. Positional thinking in non-monetary terms over time also embraces the 'holistic' idea of economics and is, as an example, very different from the monetary discounting idea of CBA. It is argued that if we are interested in the 'welfare' or the 'wealth' of individuals and nations, it would be an excellent idea to focus (mainly) on non-monetary states or positions over time. The Worldwatch Institute in

Washington, DC, is on the right path in trying to ascertain whether 'the state of the world' is (or is not) worsening in different respects (Worldwatch Institute, 1997). This question can be broken down into specific ecosystems, specific species, and so on. Similarly, we may ask questions about the health status or social position of individuals. Is the position, say in educational terms, improving or not for a specific category of people? Another characteristic of PA, which could also perhaps have been used as a basis for the designation, has to do with our PEP assumptions, the imperatives of democracy and the ideas about management and conflict analysis connected with the approach.

PURPOSE AND CONTEXT OF STUDIES

We have already made a distinction between studies oriented towards the past, the present and the future. Many studies cover two of these temporal aspects and some cover all three; but the emphasis is usually on only one.

Some studies have their focus, or at least starting point, in technology. So-called 'technology assessment' has been carried out since the late 1970s, where specific 'new' and 'old' technologies (nuclear energy, supersonic aircraft technology and so on) have been made the subject of investigation with respect to expected environmental and other impacts. LCA with its 'from-cradle-to-grave' perspective focuses primarily on products rather than technology, although the two are of course interrelated. Some studies focus on a specific category of impacts. Examples here are EIA, social impact assessment (SIA), see Becker, 1997) and perhaps also monetary impact assessment (MIA), a new and more appropriate name for something which has always been very close to the hearts of economists and many others. Some of us emphasize impact studies that are all inclusive – a concept sometimes referred to as integrated impact assessment (IIA) (Rossini and Porter, 1983, Cornland, personal communication, 1997). PA belongs to this 'all-inclusive' category.

Most of the methods and approaches mentioned above focus on ongoing activities and alternatives for the future. A holistic concept of economics is often preferred in the sense that impacts are presented in highly disaggregated forms, but the 'engineering habit' of looking for a single best alternative through one-dimensional calculation is sometimes apparent, for instance when LCA is carried out.

As suggested in Table 6.1, approaches differ with respect to organizational and institutional context and the analyst's viewpoint. A study may be carried out within an organization (for instance a business corporation or a university), by someone employed by the organization. Such a study may either focus on past activities, present activities or future activities or some combination of these (Table 6.1). EMSs such as EMAS and ISO 14001 primarily concern ongoing and future activities. These approaches are based on a specific management philosophy and involve the environmental policy of the organization as well as more routinized activities. In fact, the main idea seems to be to change a consciousness about the environment by adding new routines to previously existing ones. New routines will in turn normally lead to some kind of modification or even extinction of previous routines and thought patterns. Consultancy may be involved, for instance when the initial environmental study or auditing is carried out by an outside organization as a normal part of a total EMS.

Table 6.1 *Classification of Studies According to an Analyst's Viewpoint and Time Aspect*

Viewpoint of analyst	Time aspect		
	RETROSPECTIVE	ONGOING	FUTURE ORIENTED
Inside organization/ administration	I	II	III
Outside, auditing	IV	V	VI
Outside, consultancy	VII	VIII	IX
Outside, university	X	XI	XII

A university may have its own internal EMS and conduct studies with the purpose of being certified according to ISO 14001 rules. But the purpose of a university is very much to critically examine what goes on elsewhere in society. In public administration, the tendency is rather to respect territories between sectors. Road planning is left to the road planning agency, while other agencies deal with forestry, agriculture, industry, etc. This means that the road planning agency can normally act from a position where other agencies only comment upon details. This is an unfortunate situation, as I see it. If it is agreed that 'values are always with us' (in other words, ideology is always involved) then a situation with a working dialogue and more than one study of the same issue becomes preferable. I believe that administrations at municipal and country levels should carry out complementary and more or less independent studies. Universities, too, could be involved in this, especially where new approaches are applied and evaluated, but such involvement should be on an ad hoc, rather than a regular basis. Some of these university studies could be retrospective, others future oriented. PA, by way of an example, has been mainly used for these two purposes.

DECISION TREES IN POSITIONAL TERMS

In Chapter 5, decision processes were discussed in terms of different kinds of commitments over time. We referred in a metaphorical sense to the opening and closing of doors. Depending on their power position, with legitimacy as one component, specific actors or stakeholders can influence when and where doors are opened or closed and thereby the outcome of a decision process. A closed door can sometimes be reopened and it was argued that the imperatives of democracy can work in the direction of opening for public scrutiny and dialogue some of the doors which might otherwise remain closed.

In this section, the development of a decision process will be described in terms of paths and as movements from one (mostly non-monetary) state or position (for a specific object of description such as a lake or other ecosystem) to another (cf Figure 6.1). The impacts of a given decision – for instance to walk to my office along a specific route – can be described as a series of positions P_0, P_1, P_2, for my body and person in geographical or spatial terms. P stands for position or state; P_0 for my position at point in time zero (for instance when my walking starts) and P_1 for my position at t_1, that is at a point in time, 1. Walking through a park, over a bridge across a river and through a housing estate, will lead to a series of perceptions of landscape, river, houses, and the whole walk or path will lead to certain experiences that I may forget quickly – or remember. Something special may happen during this walk, or it may be just an ordinary promenade between home and office. During my walk, I will adapt to an environment with numerous facilitating physical arrangements, for instance a pathway through a park, a bridge and a road or street, but also barriers. There may be parts of the park which I do not want to cross for one reason or other. It may be wise to cross the river where the bridge is located, although I may have to mingle with motor traffic to use the bridge. I cannot walk across private gardens, as I prefer to observe certain rules for decent behaviour that I feel exist in this neighborhood.

The path that I follow may develop into a habit that I perceive as good or bad for body and mind – for my health, in broad terms. But I may occasionally choose a different path because it is quicker, but less enjoyable. If I walk close to the road with sometimes heavy motor traffic, noise and pollution will not leave me totally unaffected. I may be exposed to noise and particles from the car exhausts, some of which

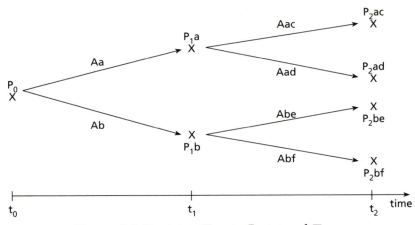

Figure 6.1 *Decision Tree in Positional Terms*

(eg lead) may be accumulating in my body. If I systematically follow one path rather than another my health may be affected differently, especially in the long run. My weight and physical fitness will perhaps change in positional terms.

This trivial story, and many others, can be related to the decision tree shown in Figure 6.1. From a starting position on a given day and hour, I make certain choices. Aa refers to one path for the first part of my move until t_1, and A_b to another path. Depending on which one of the alternatives I choose, I will be in different positions, P_1a and P_1b respectively, at time t_1 and these positions will in turn represent different initial positions and thereby influence the options for the rest of my walk. Should I pass the park in some longer, but more pleasant way, or should I choose the shortest pathway? I may have additional options at some stages and places.

Not only impacts on people, but also on the environment, can be interpreted and described in positional terms. Building houses, roads, factories and so on, where there were forests and open landscape before, will mean changes in land use patterns that are not easily – if ever – reversible. Mercury pollution from a pulp mill can affect different components in a nearby ecosystem, for instance a lake. Mercury accumulates in fish and can be measured over time as the content of mercury in fish caught at a particular place.

The idea behind decision trees of the kind depicted in Figure 6.1 is to suggest that a decision process and its outcome can be seen as a multiple stage process. Often the choice between options at a point in time will not lead to a unique series of positions in the future, but rather to many possible series of positions. The chess player chooses her or his first move which opens (and closes) possibilities for the

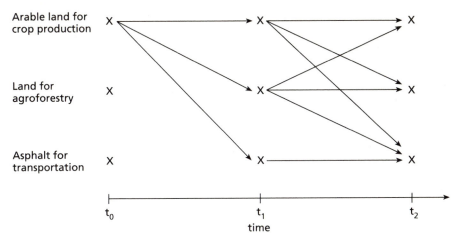

Figure 6.2 *Decision Tree Applied to Qualitative Changes in Land Use*

future and the same is true of decisions concerning land use, the choice between production techniques in a factory, or the choice of courses and educational programmes for a student.

As suggested by the examples, 'positions' can be of a qualitative or quantitative kind and a position may refer to one object of description, or many (for instance different components in a lake's ecosystem). Each object of description may furthermore be described in one-dimensional or multidimensional terms. The decision tree in Figure 6.2 shows positional changes of a primarily qualitative kind. Consider a particular plot of land initially (at t_0) used for crop production. Two alternative uses for the same plot are being considered. One is to move from crop production to agroforestry, which would affect the structure and content of the soil, but leave the biological productivity of the land essentially unaffected. The second alternative refers to a proposal of the national road planning agency to build a road on the same piece of land. Planners at the agency argue that the best route for the road happens to pass through our farmer's land.

Let us furthermore assume that the time distance between t_0 and t_1 (and between t_1 and t_2) in Figure 6.2 is 3 years and that this time allows movements:

- from crop production to agroforestry;
- from crop production to asphalted road; and
- from agroforestry back to crop production.

Once the road has been constructed however, it is not possible to return either to crop production, or to agroforestry. For practical purposes, the asphalting process is seen as an irreversible change in land use. (No arrows point back to agroforestry or crop production from asphalted surface in Figure 6.2.) Horizontal arrows suggest that continuing with the same land use for the next period is always an option.

Quantification is also relevant in many situations. Let us return to the case of mercury as a pollutant. In Figure 6.3, the outflow of mercury (in kilograms per year) from a pulp-mill to a nearby lake is illustrated on the left vertical axis, while the positional aspect, the mercury content in fish (measured in milligrams of mercury per kilogram (parts per million – ppm) of fish caught at a particular place in the lake), is measured along the right vertical axis.

In the case illustrated, the outflow of mercury from the mill was 20 kg for the years 1995, 1996 and 1997. As a result of this, the ppm level of mercury in fish has been increasing. The mercury outflow from the mill can be controlled – at some monetary cost – and it is assumed that three alternatives are being considered. One is to continue as before with 20 kg per year (cf A_0). In this case the mercury content in fish (as measured on the right-hand side) increases to even higher levels than before. According to alternative A_1, the outflow is reduced to 15 kg per year rather than the previous 20 kg. In this case too, an increase in the mercury content in fish is anticipated. This is, as I see it, an important point in understanding many environmental problems. Reduction in a flow variable is certainly better than an increase, but the reduction may be insufficient to achieve an improvement in positional terms.

In the present case the properties of mercury as a heavy metal are a significant factor. Alternative A_2 represents a more radical reduction of the outflow of mercury from the pulp mill. In this case, a slight reduction (and thereby improvement) in the mercury content in fish is expected, that is a slowly decreasing ppm level.

The three different versions of our decision tree (Figures 6.1, 6.2, 6.3) point to the importance of inertia. Inertia exists on many dimensions, such as cognitive, affective, behavioural, institutional, physical, biological, etc. Complete flexibility in moving between states (positions) appears to be the exception rather than the normal case. Many environmental impacts represent serious problems because of irreversibility, that is a difficulty in returning to a previous position (agricultural land, unpolluted groundwater). On the other hand there may also be positive examples of inertia from an environmental point of view, for instance when knowledge has been accumulated about environmentally more friendly technologies and behavioural patterns. Some human thought patterns and habits of people play a positive rather than negative role.

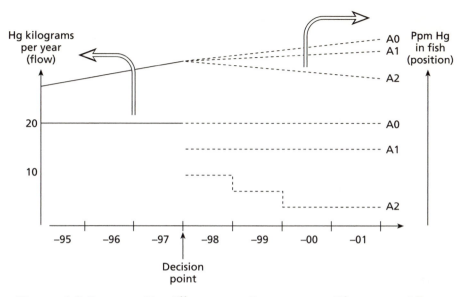

Figure 6.3 *Decision Tree Illustrating Quantitative Changes, ie How Mercury Pollution (a flow variable) is Estimated to Affect Fish in Terms of Mercury Content (a Positional Variable)*

Another term which appears in the recent literature and which fits well into our decision trees and examples is 'path dependence' (see North, 1990; Magnusson and Ottosson, 1997). We are in a sense 'locked into' specific ways of thinking, specific behaviour patterns or life-styles, specific technologies and institutional arrangements such as a version of the capitalistic system. Change is not always possible and when it is possible it will often be marginal, that is to say it will be quite limited change.

One practical conclusion for the purposes of decision-making is that a focus on inertia and the identification of irreversible impacts is often a good idea. Making an effort to do this is an important part of a scheme of analysis for PA studies, as we will see.

COMPARING ALTERNATIVES WITH RESPECT TO IMPACTS AND CONFLICTS OF INTEREST

Some decision situations can be described as simple, while others are more complex. A decision situation is relatively simple if:

- only one individual is the decision maker;
- only the individual her- or himself is expected to be affected;
- the individual has a clear ideological orientation;

- expected impacts are certain, rather than uncertain;
- at least one alternative exists whose impacts closely match the individual's ideological orientation;
- the individual has had positive experiences when making similar choices in the past.

A decision situation is more complex:

- the larger the number of decision makers;
- the more individuals and/or organizations that are affected and can therefore be seen as stakeholders;
- the more individuals involved who are uncertain about their ideological orientation in relation to the decision situation (individuals may for instance perceive conflicts between their various motives and interests);
- the more uncertain impacts are, especially the 'more important' impacts;
- the more the ideological orientation differs among decision makers as one category and among stakeholders as another category.

Simple decision situations in the above sense are not without interest from a scientific point of view, but they are usually easily handled by the individual and there is less need for outside help and specific decision support techniques.

Problems related to the environment and development are in most cases rather complex in relation to the dimensions listed. In the typical case there are many decision makers and stakeholders who furthermore differ considerably with respect to their attitude to risk and other parts of their ideological orientation.

Much can be done to facilitate dialogue. Outsiders may enter the process as mediators, organizational arrangements may facilitate constructive dialogue and rapprochement between decision makers and stakeholders. But some disagreement will remain, nevertheless. The questions that will be addressed here are: first, whether it is desirable to make disagreement visible to decision makers (for instance, politicians) and secondly, how this can be done.

It is probably not difficult to find politicians and other decision makers who want to know as little as possible about the losers and how they are affected when one alternative is chosen as opposed to another. For them, the CBA idea of only one aggregated societal interest is very attractive. Other politicians may prefer an open discussion about ideologies and about both losers and winners.

We have to return here to the imperatives of democracy previously presented. Even if a majority of politicians and other decision makers were to prefer an analysis that conceals the losers in a decision situation, this is no reason for choosing CBA or other approaches that counteract our imperatives of democracy. Economists, as experts, should not participate by legitimizing CBA and other methods that are not compatible with democracy.

There appear to be three main ways to deal with conflicting interests:

- interviews with decision makers, stakeholders and other actors by 'inside analysts' or by engaging analysts from a more independent organization;
- arranging a dialogue between stakeholders, decision makers and other actors, for instance in the form of 'round table' meetings, public hearings and the like;
- complementary technical approaches, for instance systematically comparing alternatives at the level of impacts and the kind of activity/interest analysis that will be described below.

Interviews – and sometimes simply conversations – with stakeholders and other actors who are knowledgeable about an issue can be a very rich source of information. Such interviews can be tape-recorded and direct citations from this material are often useful as a means to understanding how the stakeholder/actor perceives the problem, what she or he feels about it, what alternatives she or he regards as relevant for further study as well as personal assessments of expected impacts. Each stakeholder may also be asked about how she or he perceives her or his own role and that of other stakeholders or actors.

The ideas and information gathered through interviews can be brought to organized meetings with analysts, stakeholders and, if possible, decision makers. Interviews and round table discussions should be arranged to assist the creative function of searching for alternatives and assessing impacts. The meetings should be documented and thereby made public.

Initiatives for round table and similar arrangements normally come from the legitimate authorities. A university scholar may be involved as a mediator or expert. In the normal case, it is not possible by someone acting from a university position to arrange meetings with many stakeholders without the consent of the authorities. One option for the university scholar, however, is to carry out a more technical analysis of the impacts and of the activities and interests that are affected. Let us assume that at some stage in the planning and interaction process, a limited set of alternatives, A_0, A_1 and A_2, has been identified for further study. These alternatives can be systematically compared at two levels: impacts and activities/interests. Three questions will be raised:

1   What systems of various kinds will be affected differently, depending on which one of the three alternatives is chosen?
2   What dimensions are relevant for a systematic comparison of the differences between the alternatives with respect to impacts?
3   What activities will be affected, depending on the option chosen and what are the interests connected with these activities?

As a first step, an attempt is made to identify those systems, S_1, S_2, S_3 ... S_n that will be affected differently, depending on which one of the considered options is chosen (cf Table 6.2). In planning a new highway, for instance, the transportation system will of course be affected, although perhaps not only the road network but also the railway network. In addition, local ecosystems, systems for agriculture and forestry may be affected as well as the atmosphere as a system (through CO_2 emissions). Commercial systems (filling stations, restaurants) in specific areas may also be affected in terms of turnover if a large part of the traffic transfers from one highway to another. The same is probably true of housing areas along the routes being considered.

Table 6.2 *Identification of Systems that are Expected to be Affected and the Spatial Extension of Impacts*

Systems	Levels of impact			
	LOCAL	REGIONAL	NATIONAL	GLOBAL
S_1	✔			
S_2	✔	✔	✔	✔
S_3	✔	✔		
S_n	✔			

The identification of affected systems should be helpful in identifying the relevant dimensions for the comparison of impacts. Impacts for each alternative can be described in both qualitative and quantitative terms. When constructing the road, land-use patterns will typically change and ecosystems will be disturbed. A new highway will inevitably cause noise and air pollution but old, previously existing roads and their environs may benefit. Qualitative and quantitative estimates of impacts for each alternative can be made on a matrix as a first step (Table 6.3). Qualitative statements may be used to summarize the comparison between A_1 and A_0 (and between A_2 and A_0) for each impact dimension, using the following scale (Table 6.4):

A_1 considerably better than A_0
A_1 somewhat better than A_0
A_1 equivalent to A_0
A_1 somewhat worse than A_0
A_1 considerably worse than A_0

Many issues can be discussed in relation to matrices or tables of this kind. How does 'considerably better' differ from 'somewhat better', for instance? The only answer that one can give is to discuss openly how these judgements have been made.

Table 6.3 *Qualitative and Quantitative Comparisons can be Made for Each Impact Dimension*

Impact dimension	Alternative A_0	A_1	A_2
I_1	–	–	–
I_2	–	–	–
I_3	–	–	–
I_k	–	–	–

Let us now move to the third question. In addition to the comparisons mentioned, alternatives can be compared at the level of activities and interests to make visible the compatibility and conflicts of interest. As in the case of systems as discussed above, the activities of the individuals and organizations, which will be affected in different ways depending on the option chosen, can be identified and listed. For each activity identified, an assumption is made about its goal direction, which in turn can be used for the ranking of alternatives from the point of view of the activity. For people living in houses close to a busy road, one may assume that they would prefer a level of environmental disturbance from the road (noise, air pollution, traffic congestion, etc) that is as low as possible. On the basis of this assumption, an option which includes the building of a new road which would divert some of the traffic will be preferred to a situation (zero alternative) with no new transportation facilities. A matrix can then be constructed as in Table 6.5 with options in the columns and the identified activities in the rows (living close to a road, transportation activities between

Table 6.4 A_1 *and* A_2 *are Both Compared with* A_0*,*
a 'No Action' Alternative

Impact dimension	Alternative A_1	A_2
I_1	equivalent to A_0	considerably better than A_0
I_2	somewhat worse than A_0	considerably worse than A_0
I_3	somewhat better than A_0	considerably better than A_0
I_k	considerably better than A_0	equivalent to A_0

specific places, agricultural activity, commercial activity in a specific area, etc).

The ranking of alternatives according to Table 6.5 depends on the assumptions made about goal direction (target orientation) for a specific activity and the reasonableness of these assumptions is always open to debate. Planners and architects make such assumptions about the needs of people and organizations when drawing their maps and sometimes standards exist, for example, for permitted levels of noise. To draw up a preference order, only a goal direction is needed, but information about the number of individuals involved in a specific activity and whether or not specific standards are observed is, of course, also relevant. In some cases, it is not always easy to separate two alternatives with respect to an activity with connected interest. The alternatives may then be given the same ranking, or a tentative ranking may be indicated by question marks as for AC_n in Table 6.5.

In the kind of complex decision situations that interest us, it is rather unusual for one alternative to be the best from the point of view of all activities and interests. In our example, A_2 is ranked number one according to three interests but is the worst alternative in relation to activity/interest 2. What is at issue is whether or not this activity/interest is important for a particular decision maker with her or his ideological orientation.

It should be noted that the ranking is based on specific activities carried out by individuals and organizations. This means that one individual or stakeholder may be affected through more than one activity and the preference orders for these different activities may differ – or may be similar. In such a situation, the individual's preferences in relation to the alternatives are a matter of her or his ideological orientation, where all activities will potentially be considered (and not only those that make the individual a stakeholder). In order to collect information about the individual's preferences in relation to the options, one has to ask her or him which takes us back to the value of interviews and round table discussions.

Table 6.5 *Activity–Interest Analysis where Compatibilities of Interest and Conflicts of Interest are Made Visible*

Activity with connected interest	Alternative A_0	A_1	A_2
AC_1	2	3	1
AC_2	1	2	3
AC_3	3	2	1
AC_n	2?	3?	1

INVESTMENT DECISIONS: A SCHEME OF ANALYSIS

This chapter can be summarized with a scheme of analysis for future oriented PA studies carried out from a university perspective:

- Describe the issue and institutional context. Make a preliminary attempt to identify stakeholders and other actors. Identify the of rules of the game, for instance the roles of different actors and stakeholders.
- Identification of problem. How do different stakeholders and other actors perceive the problem? Try to find out the historical background to the present decision situation. Do previous studies exist?
- Make a creative effort to generate possible alternatives of choice by listening to stakeholders and in other ways.
- Formulate the problem for the purposes of analysis, for instance by choosing those alternatives that will be investigated further. Three or four alternatives are recommended and they should differ in kind in the sense that they should respond to different possible ideological orientations. Perform an analysis of how the present decision situation relates to other decision situations, for instance at the strategic or policy level.
- Carry out a disaggregated analysis where monetary and non-monetary impacts are kept separate and where the distinction between flows and positions is observed.
- Identify systems that will be affected differently depending on the alternative chosen.
- Make a systematic comparison of alternatives with respect to impacts in both qualitative and quantitative terms.
- Conduct a special study of inertia and irreversible impacts that will influence future options in positional and other terms.

- Activity–interest analysis. Identify the activities for individuals and organizations that will be affected differently depending on the alternative chosen. Rank the options on the basis of assumptions about goal direction for each activity.
- Perform an analysis of risk and uncertainty, for instance with reference to scenarios. Assumptions can be made about the development path of various uncertain variables (such as future prices of oil in a study of bioenergy and other alternative fuels).
- Articulate the different ideological orientations (ideas about development and progress) that appear to be relevant for decision makers and stakeholders.
- Draw conditional conclusions in relation to alternative ideological orientations and scenarios.

It should be emphasized that it is possible and often fruitful to move back and forth between the different points in this scheme and one need not necessarily follow this proposal strictly in making a study. The institutional context for the analyst may be such that it is possible to involve stakeholders more in the analysis than is suggested by this particular scheme.

ANALYSIS OF ONGOING ACTIVITIES AND RETROSPECTIVE PA

While there has been an emphasis on future oriented PA so far, it is argued that much of the political economics approach presented is also applicable for ongoing activities and for follow-up studies. This is true of the holistic idea of economics described in Chapter 4, as well as the distinctions between monetary and non-monetary impacts and between flows and positions. In Figure 4.2, changes in efficiency were discussed for one activity from one period to another, as well as changes in positional terms connected with these activities. Focusing on one activity is not enough when addressing environmental issues and LCA was discussed as a way of linking activities (which are often carried out in different organizations) to one another.

Follow-up studies, as the name suggests, may focus on comparisons between:

- actual performance for one period compared with actual performance in the preceding period;
- actual performance for a specific period, compared with previously expected performance.

In the case of 'retrospective PA', the idea in the past has often been to follow up investment decisions. Politicians in one municipality, Kil in the county of Värmland, made the decision to invest in bioenergy early in the 1970s. Pellets were used rather than oil. At the time of the investment decision, there was considerable uncertainty about future oil prices and environmental charges on oil. In this case, the bioenergy pathway was compared with a hypothetical pathway for Kil with an energy system based on oil, similar to neighbouring municipalities. It was concluded that the series of investments made in an energy system based on forest fuel had led to an improved level of environmental performance, while at the same time being no more expensive in terms of monetary costs (Forsberg, 1993).

In another study, state financial support for so-called 'tree section systems' to increase the use of forest fuel was followed up with the use of retrospective PA (Hillring, 1996). The plans and expectations at the time of applying for support were compared with the actual outcomes. Some of these facilities were still in use ten years later, but others had closed. As an additional source of information, interviews were held with representatives of those organizations that had originally applied for financial support.

My own conclusion from this is that follow-up studies of different kinds are as interesting and thought provoking as future oriented studies and that more can be done in terms of systematic attempts to learn from past experience. Another question that can be raised is why one sees so little of 'retrospective CBA'. The past appears to be irrelevant as part of the CBA methodology and other neo-classical analysis, where concepts such as 'sunk costs' belong to the mind set.

Chapter 7

A Policy for Ecological Sustainability

In Chapter 6, it was argued that inertia is a characteristic not only of physical and biological change, but also of social and institutional processes. Reference was made to 'path dependence'. We are in many ways 'locked into' specific development paths. Our present political–economic system, where democracy is combined with a form of market capitalism, is not easily changed. And there are many who see no reason for change, but in fact perceive the present situation as the best of all possible worlds. For them, continuing along the present development path presents few problems.

If all citizens were happy with the present development path, inertia as a phenomenon would not be much of a problem. 'Nothing succeeds like success' as Armen Alchian once wrote when discussing theories of the firm (Alchian, 1950). If all agree that there is success at the micro- as well as the macro-level, this success could very well continue. Inertia becomes more of a problem when an increasing proportion of the population find themselves unhappy with present development trends and refers to criteria which allow them to see numerous examples of failure rather than success. Differences in ideological orientation can explain variations in the success criteria that different groups apply.

This study does not claim value neutrality for the reasons explained in Chapter 2. We are interested in success criteria that reflect 'ecological sustainability' and seek strategies and policies that will facilitate social change and advance in that direction. With this particular set of success indicators in mind, not only failure but also success can be reported. Environmental labelling (and consequent change in consumer behaviour) is one example, EMS (which in a gradual manner is expected to lead to improved environmental performance in business) is another.

In the present chapter we will suggest answers to two kinds of question:

1   How do societies change? What explanatory models for societal change could be of assistance?
2   How can change in the direction of improved environmental performance at micro- and macro-levels be encouraged and facilitated?

In the first section we will discuss principles, strategies and instruments of social change from the point of view of important actor categories, such as state agencies, business corporations, citizen environmental organizations (CeOs) and universities.

How do Societies Change?

A number of models claim to explain societal change. These models can often be seen as complementary, that is mutually supportive. Some can be connected with specific disciplines. Each model identifies specific actions and instruments as meaningful in the attempt to influence development. The list of models given here is meant to suggest a number of possibilities, but in no way claims to be complete.

The Paradigm and Ideology Development Model

The overall model of this book is concerned with paradigms and ideologies. In some sense this model covers all other models to be described. It is argued that paradigms do matter as part of the sustainability discourse and that each paradigm is specific, not only in conceptual terms but also in ideological terms. Different paradigms within a single discipline such as economics will point in different directions when explaining how societies change (Figure 7.1). Different ways of perceiving and formulating the problems in turn lead to different development strategies, or ways of tackling problems.

Paradigm A in Figure 7.1 may stand for neo-classical economics, which points in the direction of a specific market model and offers 'solutions' to problems by suggesting environmental charges, tax schemes and sometimes institutionally designed markets for 'pollution permits' – so-called 'bubble markets'. Our political–economics approach, which can be described as an institutional version of ecological economics, includes market models of a slightly different kind and points to a much broader range of models, as will be indicated here.

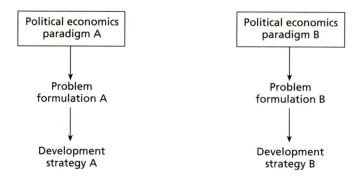

Figure 7.1 *Paradigms and Associated Ideologies are Suggested as Important Explanations of Societal Change*

The Learning and Education Model

Just as the development and articulation of paradigms and ideologies is an essential approach to ecological sustainability, the same can be said of learning and educational activities. As an example, all the EMS previously referred to involve short courses in environmental management for all members of an organization.

Learning can take place in a variety of ways and need not be connected with specific courses. As one example of a learning model which claims to explain how behaviour may change, we may refer to 'rewards' and 'penalties' or punishments. These can be non-monetary as well as monetary and the former need be no less important than the latter (Table 7.1). Behaving in a particular way sometimes leads to rewards and punishments of all four kinds according to the table, while in other cases perhaps only one of the categories in the table is relevant.

Table 7.1 *Some Behaviour Alternatives are Rewarded, Other Alternatives are Punished and these Rewards/Punishments may be Monetary or Non-Monetary in Kind*

	Reward	Penalty
Monetary	I	II
Non-monetary	III	IV

The Social Movement Model

Scholars of political science and sociology may point to the importance of social movements in changing societies. Environmental movements, which tend to differ in the number of their members and in their strategies, have played and are playing an important role in guiding development in more environmentally friendly directions.

In Sweden, social movements of a different kind have historically been of significance, for instance in transforming the country into a so-called welfare society. Workers in industry and the public sector, together with an element of the 'intelligentsia', organized themselves politically in the Social Democratic Party and also controlled the labour unions. In this way, they improved the conditions of the working class and 'solidarity' became a key concept. In Sweden, social movements of this kind are called *folkrörelser*, that is 'people's movements'. In his book *Green Political Thought* (1995), Andrew Dobson discusses whether environmental issues could lead to the formation of such movements and organizations with a certain broadness and strength. Could some underprivileged class be identified which would 'unite' and thereby increase its political and other power? Those who suffer more than others from the present development path are perhaps younger people (who too often see their parents and other adults behave as if there were no environmental problems at all) and, of course, future generations.

As many other European countries, Sweden has a Green political party which is an important step. But individuals may be 'green' in their ideological orientation while being members of other political parties and, indeed, without being members of any political party at all. This 'greening' phenomenon may refer to individuals in many different roles, for instance as concerned citizens and as professionals. And within each such category identified (engineer, economist, etc), a distinction can be made between those who are 'green' in their orientation and those who are 'non-green'.

Let us return awhile to the concept of a 'people's movement'. 'The people' are often seen as being opposed to the 'establishment' – the 'ruling class' – or those who are in power in the sense that they can influence development at the societal level on the basis of their professional, political or other positions. The 'establishment' is seen as consisting of actors who permit only marginal and controlled changes and who are largely in favour of the status quo, while change is seen as being initiated by 'the people' and their social movements.

Let us now assume that all individuals in Sweden (or any other country) can be described as either belonging to 'the people' or 'the establishment'. We furthermore assume that the same population can be divided into a 'Green' and a 'non-Green' category (cf Figure 7.2). This means that we have four categories of individuals:

t_0

ENG	EG
PNG	PG

t_1

ENG	EG
PNG	PG

Figure 7.2 *In Addition to People's Movements of a Green Kind, there may be 'Establishment Movements' in the Same Direction*

- people, green (PG);
- people, non-green (PNG);
- establishment, Green (EG);
- establishment, non-Green (ENG).

Changes in the size, both absolute and relative, of all these categories can take place between two points in time. In Figure 7.2 we are speculating about the situation at two points in time, first in 1972, at the time of the Stockholm United Nations Conference on the Human Environment, and secondly, the situation in the year 2000. For simplicity, we assume that the total population is the same in AD2000 as it was in 1972 and that the proportion (and number) of individuals belonging to 'the establishment' is unchanged. Contrary to simplistic views about people (as agents of change) and establishment (as a barrier to change), it is assumed here that some part of the establishment are in favour of a Green society and that some part of the 'people' are, for one reason or other, against such a Green development.

According to my scattered observations, the number of 'establishment actors' in business, public agencies and also (but perhaps at a slower rate) in universities, who are 'seriously Green', appears to be increasing steadily in Sweden. We now see phenomena such as the Natural Step, which can be described as an 'establishment environmental organization', financially supported by business and acting with a co-operative and non-confrontational dialogue strategy in relation to business (see below for further details). EMAS and ISO 14001 are other forces at play and at least three political parties are pushing in the same direction (the Green Party, the Centre Party and, increasingly, the Social Democrats). Only the Moderate Party (Conservatives) appear to lag behind.

By the year 2000, we may be in a situation where even the more 'opportunistically inclined' establishment actors have become 'Green' and perhaps also a situation where the establishment is 'more Green' than the people in proportional terms (Figure 7.2). This is no doubt wishful thinking, but my 'hypothesis' about the future is not completely without foundation in terms of empirical fact. Whatever the case, people's movements and establishment movements will both play a role in the success or failure of the official objectives to transform society in a Green direction.

Public Choice and Actor–Network Models

Public choice theory was introduced in Chapter 3. This is a theory which identifies specific actor categories in society, such as farmers, bureaucrats (civil servants) and politicians, and which sees social change as a question of power and competition between farmers as an interest group, bureaucrats as an interest group and so on. Small groupings with relatively homogeneous interests are expected to be more successful in organizing themselves and conducting lobbying activities. Their shares of total incomes in a country will be quite high when compared with other less homogeneous groups.

Public choice theory can be seen as an extension and modification of the neo-classical paradigm. In addition to consumers and firms, actor categories referring to different professions, such as 'farmers' and 'bureaucrats' enter the scene. Assumptions are made about a kind of 'collective egoism' connected with 'rent-seeking' activities and shares of the total 'income cake' in a country. As was mentioned in Chapter 3, the theory predicts that farmers will be relatively successful in this struggle between interest groups, while environmental interests will not be so easily organized.

Public choice theory is admittedly attractive in some respects. Representatives of interest groups influence the outcomes of policy discourse in Stockholm or Brussels (for instance concerning agricultural policy) and their lobbying activities may be based on rather narrow goals. (The theory actually tends to legitimize such narrowness.) As we will see, the assumed narrowness of the goals and the unwillingness to consider broader ideological issues is a weakness of the theory.

If ideology is taken seriously, then the assumed homogeneity of farmers as an interest group breaks down, at least in the Swedish context. Just as was the case with our previous discussion about the 'establishment', there is a 'Green' subset of farmers in Sweden (organized as 'ecological farmers' belonging to the KRAV organization) and another, 'non-Green' subset. Neither group is alone in the struggle for their own vision of a future society. Green farmers can build networks and coalitions with 'Green' bureaucrats, 'Green' politicians and, more generally, with 'non-farmers' who are 'Green'. As part of this actor network theory, which builds on PEP assumptions, one need

t_0	
FNG	FG
NFNG	NFG

t_1	
FNG	FG
NGNG	NFG

Figure 7.3 *Farmers as well as 'All Others' (ie 'Non-Farmers')*
can be Divided into Green and non-Green. The Actor–Network
Approach thereby Suggests a Different Classification of Actor
Categories or Interest Groups in Society

no longer be pessimistic about the future of environmental interests.
What will happen depends on a whole set of factors and cannot be
deduced from any simple theory.

Figure 7.3 follows the same logic as Figure 7.2. We are dealing with
the following subcategories of the entire total population:

- farmers, Green (FG);
- farmers, non-Green (FNG);
- non-farmers, Green (NFG);
- non-farmers, non-Green (NFNG).

The numbers of individuals in each category may change from one
point in time, t_0, to another, t_1, as suggested in the figure. In our
example, the Green part (FG + NFG) of the whole population is
increasing over time. Other developments are also possible of course,
for instance a reduction in the total number of individuals who qualify
as Green. The important point here is to realize that the
actor–network view prepares the way for an economics where ideological debate and democracy matter and, one may add, a less cynical
economics (cf Söderbaum 1991, 1992).

Organizational and Institutional Models

Will institutional arrangements in an organization, municipality, or
country hinder or facilitate changes in some desired direction? Recent
EMSs normally place the emphasis on necessary organizational
changes, for instance in the sense that responsibilities for environmental performance are allocated among individuals. Changes in the
organizational design of public agencies are often considered in an
attempt to come to grips with complex problems. Even CeOs or
universities may reorganize and reallocate resources as a way of matching what is happening elsewhere in society.

In studies on governmental policy, state intervention and legislation is often considered as a way of dealing with specific problems. New laws entail new 'rules of the game'. Will penalties for environmental damage also be very limited in the future when compared with other kinds of non-compliance, suggesting that 'society' does not take such damage seriously?

A general strengthening of democracy within an organization, a municipality or a country, may be another way to improve performance which makes it relevant to refer to a 'democracy model' of social change. Agenda 21 activities in Swedish municipalities can be seen as an attempt to emphasize a 'bottom-up' rather than a 'top-down' strategy (cf Ministry of Environment, 1997). This echoes our emphasis on the 'imperatives of democracy' (Chapter 5).

In addition to state intervention, there are 'voluntary' models of social change. Trade organizations may put pressure on member companies to improve their environmental performance in the interests of industry as a whole. Here the 'Responsible Care Programme' applied within the chemicals industry in some countries is an often cited example (Simmons and Wynne, 1993). Industrialists may prefer a more proactive role instead of one where ambitions stop at compliance. The World Business Council for Sustainable Development (WBCSD) discussed in Chapter 4 can be seen as a trade organization at the international level, specializing in international affairs and suggesting conceptual frameworks and practical means of improving the environmental performance of member companies.

Another example of voluntary arrangements is 'partnerships' between municipalities for co-operative learning purposes and as a way of recognizing, for instance, that environmental performance on the other side of the Baltic is also important from a Swedish point of view. The Stockholm Water Company is co-operating with Latvia's Riga Water Company for this reason.

One important dimension in all this appears to be confrontation versus co-operation. While state control is still essential, a 'new' role for governmental agencies as facilitators of desired change appears to be increasing in importance. The government can also utilize its powers of market intervention in order to improve the environmental performance of products such as refrigerators and road vehicles (NUTEK, 1993).

Market Models

Market models can be seen as a subset of the 'organization and institutional models' referred to above. Here, the neo-classical supply and demand model is one subcategory and the actor–network model of markets discussed in Chapter 3 is another. The former emphasizes competition, the latter co-operation. It is clear that 'ideological orientation', heading in a Green direction, will influence not only the purchasing activities of consumers but also the purchasing practices of businesses and municipalities. A corporation may put pressure on suppliers to respond to environmental criteria and more generally to move in a Green direction. A municipality could introduce environmental considerations as part of monetary budgeting processes and activities – so-called 'Green budgeting'. Suppliers may engage in Green marketing activities etc.

As we reach the end of the 20th century, there is no doubt that markets of different kinds play a significant role and constitute perhaps the most important force in transforming society. There is a potential for Green activities but, so far, markets tend to represent a destructive force in relation to ecosystems (eg tropical forest in Asia, or old growth forest in Scandinavia).

As argued earlier (Chapter 3), markets should not be regarded as an 'ethical free zone'. The ideological orientation of each market actor is of importance as well as the institutional arrangements with its systems of rules. Markets should, as I see it, be judged in terms of justice, distribution, responsibilities and other ethical concepts and less in mechanistic terms. Prices are a matter of 'fairness' and 'appropriateness' in relation to specific ideologies and ethical principles. Similarly, one may refer to 'reasonable profit' rather than maximum profit. John R Commons and many of his followers among institutional economists refer to 'administered prices' and 'reasonable prices' to point out that prices are set by individuals in specific social and institutional contexts and that their ideas about prices are always open to examination (eg Ramstad, 1987). Will the price of water at a place in Israel or of timber from a tropical rainforest be regarded as reasonable from the point of view of all interested parties, that is to say not only the seller and the buyer but also other stakeholders, including future generations?

To respond to this question is admittedly not easy. Neither is it good procedure to assume away all aspects of complexity. The best one can do is probably to illuminate the issue in a many-sided way and to articulate the ethical and ideological standpoints that appear to be relevant and appropriate to this particular consideration.

Accounting and Reporting Models

Measurement of performance in environmental, social and health-related terms is no less important than monetary accounting. EMAS,

ISO 14001 and similar environmental management systems all emphasize the need to know whether things are improving or not. In view of the multidimensional character of environmental and other non-monetary impacts, this is no easy matter. Principles for dealing with these issues were discussed in Chapters 3 and 6.

EMAS, as one among a number of EMSs, requires open access to essential information on the environmental performance of specific production (or other) facilities and the organization as a whole.

Labelling and Listing Models

Various models for gathering information about the environmental qualities of products, chemicals, etc have been developed. Industry may co-operate with state agencies concerning 'environmental labelling' programmes, or environmental organizations may by themselves develop such systems.

An example of a policy which relates to chemicals is the listing of chemicals with carcinogenic and other toxic properties to inform producers, consumers and citizens (cf Ministry of Environment, 1997).

Models for Evaluation from the Outside

It is essential for an organization to develop its own systems for environmental control, but in addition, different kinds of outside control and evaluation should be encouraged. Models for the regular auditing of environmental performance by independent organizations can be helpful, as can other kinds of interaction with outsiders as part of a learning process. Again, EMAS and ISO 14000 are relevant examples.

The Demonstration and Technology Model

It is often argued that one needs 'good examples', that is individuals and organizations who can combine knowledge from different sources and act as 'environmental entrepreneurs'. Such entrepreneurs are ready to experiment with both old and new technologies or can initiate new activities. Not only may products and technologies be innovative, but so also, for instance, can educational programmes and new institutional arrangements. Specific organizations and countries may take the lead in finding ways to improve environmental performance.

ETHICAL ISSUES AND PRINCIPLES

Problems related to the environment and development raise many ethical issues. Ethics can be seen as an essential part of ideology and ideological orientation. How do I, as an individual, relate to other contemporary or future individuals? How do we, who now live in the town of Uppsala, relate to future inhabitants of this town? How do we relate to contemporary and future individuals outside Uppsala who may be affected by our behaviour? How do we relate to other life forms or to ecosystems? Does a tree or a forest have an 'intrinsic value' and what is the meaning of intrinsic value? Is it meaningful to articulate 'ecological imperatives' for public policy in an attempt to get a more precise idea of 'ecological sustainability'?

The Brundtland report (World Commission, 1987) was not the first to discuss development concepts which incorporate environmental considerations. In the early 1970s, 'qualitative growth' was suggested in an attempt to modify simplistic welfare ideas in terms of GDP. Later, Ignacy Sachs proposed 'eco-development' (Sachs, 1976, 1984) with 'self-reliance' as one of the key concepts. Self-reliance refers to an attempt to counteract the trends toward the internationalization and globalization of trade. The eco-development concept has also been emphasized in more recent studies (Ehrenfeld, 1995).

In the early 1980s, I proposed a set of 'ecological imperatives for public policy' (Söderbaum, 1980, 1982). The idea is to think in terms of planning decisions for a municipality, such as Uppsala, and to focus on the natural resource base or position within, as well as outside of Uppsala, now and in the future. Will specific projects, programmes or policies considered for decision-making – for instance in the field of transportation (or energy systems) – lead to a degradation of the natural resource base within and outside the municipality? The following ethical considerations could then be applied:

1 Alternatives (or options) that lead to irreversible degradation of the natural resource base within the region should be avoided.
2 Alternatives that represent a shifting of the burden on the natural resource base and ecosystems onto areas outside the region should be avoided.
3 In situations of uncertainty with respect to significant irreversible negative impacts upon the natural resource base within or outside the region, a precautionary principle should be applied. A typical case is a low probability for a large-scale degradation of the natural resource base.

4 Only alternatives with a neutral or beneficial effect on the natural resource base should be considered further (with respect to other kinds of impacts). If there are no such options, a search for new alternatives should be initiated.

Imperatives 1 and 2 refer to individuals belonging to the present and future generations within and outside the region, respectively. The guiding principle is non-degradation of the natural resource position as measured in non-monetary terms. It is clear that many of our conventional 'solutions' to problems do not qualify as being environmentally friendly in the above sense.

The same ecological imperatives can be applied at the level of products or specific chemicals manufactured and sold by a corporation, or at the level of national policy concerning chemicals. In Sweden, a substitution principle has been adopted which can be regarded as one among many applications of the precautionary principle (Ministry of Environment, 1997, p84). When two pesticides are equally effective in relation to weeds but one is expected to be significantly less dangerous in health or environmental terms, then that one should replace the other.

Our ecological imperatives are formulated in we–they terms, that is for collectives of individuals. They refer both to those who live within the region, and to those who live outside it and may potentially be affected. Reasoning in terms of ethics in this way, means that one can hold politicians or others responsible for things that go wrong. It may be even more interesting to focus on specific individuals and how they regard their personal responsibilities. Lönngren and Axelsson (1995) identified 18 environmental actors representing various parts of Swedish society. Politicians and administrators on both national and municipal levels, representatives of private business, labour unions, voluntary environmental organizations, journalists – all were approached in tape-recorded interviews in the following way:

- You are active in the environmental field and you understand as well as we do how important these issues are.
- What is your vision for the future with respect to the environmental issues that you are dealing with?
- What can you do in your capacity and position to improve the situation?
- Can you identify factors that either facilitate or hinder your activities in support of an environmentally sound development?

Among the results of these interviews, some stood out as more striking than others. A considerable number of the actors interviewed admitted that the results so far of trying to reduce natural resource degradation were meagre in many ways. In explaining why, they tended to blame others. Politicians tended to see themselves as relatively innocent, while blaming industry and vice versa. On the basis of this, Lönngren and Axelsson referred to a 'responsibility trap', implying that A puts all responsibility on B, while B tends to blame A. Another version of such a trap is that A blames B while B in turn blames C. A factory worker may have suspicions about certain chemicals being used (and may know of ways to avoid these chemicals) but perhaps chooses to blame the works manager who, in turn, points to the monetary expectations of shareholders and puts all the blame on them.

A way out of this is to speak of and apply 'extended responsibility' rather than limited responsibility. In Germany and Sweden, producer responsibilities have been extended to cover the 'take back' and recycling stage of some products. Also for individuals and organizations in other roles an extended responsibility could be a way of modifying our thinking about environmental problems.

Any debate about responsibility has to be related to the present institutional context. The market economy functions largely as a way of increasing risk taking in society and to diminish responsibility. Institutional reforms may be required to make extended responsibility a realistic option. One of the first institutionalists, Thorstein Veblen, wrote about problems with 'absentee ownership', for instance shareholders who live far away from the factories they 'own'.

However, rhetoric is seldom enough. The meaning of extended responsibility must be expressed in clear terms. The 'polluter pays' principle is one such ethical principle. This principle speaks a language which is understood in business and to the extent that it is implemented, it represents an improvement.

WHO ARE THE POLICY MAKERS?

Policy is often interpreted as state intervention at the national level. In neo-classical environmental economics, the focus tends to be on various instruments that can be applied by the state. Environmental charges are a form of indirect intervention, it is argued, while other laws may directly regulate permitted levels of pollution or stipulate how ecosystems and national parks should be protected. According to this interpretation, environmental policy is something exclusively for the Ministry of Environment on the national level and perhaps also for the Commissioner for Environment at the EU level.

This view is not without relevance, but appears narrow in more than one way. First, it is very difficult to make a clear distinction between environmental policy with its associated instruments, and other policy. Agricultural policy is at the same time also environmental policy; transport policy is environmental policy, and so on. Therefore, other ministries or parts of the national government are also 'environmental policy makers'. Secondly, the role of the state in environmental affairs is no longer limited to regulation and control. As we have already alluded, the state may act on markets to improve environmental performance in much the same way as national administrations – the Water Power Board (Vattenfall) and the administration for telecommunications – acted in the past when procuring efficient plant and equipment. The state also plays its part in technological development by supporting specific kinds of research and as an opinion leader by encouraging and legitimizing specific kinds of action.

Thirdly, municipalities or local governments, for instance so-called 'eco-municipalities', may articulate an environmental policy and consider various ways to implement it.

Fourthly, an increasing number of business companies and other organizations refer to their environmental policy and must therefore be counted among the policy makers. An environmental policy is required as part of EMAS, ISO 14001 and other similar systems. Any university that wishes to become certified according to these systems has to present its environmental policy. (It may be noted that as part of neo-classical microeconomics, it becomes difficult to conceive of the firm as a 'policy maker'. The firm and the industry is seen as 'reactive', that is it responds to new state legislation by compliance and nothing more. As prices or other rules change, profit maximization simply suggests a new optimum.)

Finally, individuals, as part of our PEP assumptions, can be conceived of as political beings and policy makers. At this level of the individual, it may be preferable, however, to refer to 'environmental action' or 'environmental work' (in Swedish *miljöarbete*) rather than policy.

STRATEGIES FOR CHANGE

Individuals can influence their future development paths at the micro-level and, to a lesser extent, development at the macro-level. They can act in all their roles, as private citizens, as professionals or as politicians. Politicians and administrators at the national, county and municipal levels are among the main players as are representatives of businesses, financial capital, citizen environmental organizations and universities. Each of these actors or players can in principle refer to each one of the 'explanatory models for social change' presented (cf Table 7.2). The outcomes in terms of future states (or positions) of the environment depend on the strategies of all actors and how they relate to each other. Will they see environmental considerations as a top priority on their agenda and act accordingly, or will they tend to soft pedal these issues?

Table 7.2 *In Principle, Actors within each Category can Refer to a Set of Social Change Models and Emphasize some more than Others in an Attempt to Influence Development at both Micro- and Macro-Levels*

Explanatory models	Actor categories				
	GOVERNMENTS	BUSINESS	CEOS	UNIVERSITIES	OTHERS
Paradigm and ideology development model	–	–	–	–	–
Learning and education model	–	–	–	–	–
Social movement model	–	–	–	–	–
Public Choice and Actor–Network model	–	–	–	–	–
Organizational and institutional model	–	–	–	–	–
Market models	–	–	–	–	–
Accounting and reporting model	–	–	–	–	–
Labelling and listing model	–	–	–	–	–
Models for evaluation from 'outside'	–	–	–	–	–
Demonstration and technology model	–	–	–	–	–
Other models	–	–	–	–	–

There is, of course, no easy answer to this question. What we know more about is our own intentions to contribute in one direction or other. In this final section, I will single out three of the main players – business corporations, CeOs and universities – and discuss options with respect to roles and strategies.

In the literature on EMSs, a distinction between 'reactive' and 'proactive' policies and strategies is often mentioned. A reactive strategy refers to a tendency to obey national laws. The firm is ready to comply with existing laws and even new laws, but complying is seen as a costly matter in monetary terms and there is no reason to do more than necessary in terms of improved environmental performance. Those who on the other hand do 'more than necessary' are applying a proactive strategy.

A slightly different classification of strategies is suggested in Table 7.3. I will refer to three degrees of internalization of environmental values in thinking and action: a 'non-eco strategy', an 'intermediate strategy', and an 'eco-strategy'. 'Eco' here stands for ecological as in 'ecological agriculture', 'ecological forestry' and so on. All organizations in a market economy consider the monetary consequences of their operations, but they may differ in the extent to which they 'internalize' social and environmental values by articulating their ethics, for instance. In the classification used in Table 7.3, I have chosen to emphasize the environmental aspect, although the social aspect may be regarded as being equally important. Those companies that follow an eco-strategy will in most cases also seriously consider other non-monetary dimensions such as social impacts, although this has to be judged in each specific case. (It is of course possible to refer to an 'eco-social' strategy rather than an eco-strategy in Table 7.3 or to make further distinctions between a 'non-eco/non-social' strategy, a 'non-eco/social' strategy, an 'eco/non-social' strategy and an 'eco/social' strategy.)

Table 7.3 *Individuals and Organizations Differ in their Strategies in Relation to Environmental Issues and in Relation to Specific other Actors or Actor Categories*

Degree to which environmental values are internalized	Relationship to specific other actor(s)	
	CONFRONTATION	*CO-OPERATION*
Non-eco	a	b
Intermediate	c	d
Eco	e	f

Another distinction can be made between 'confrontation' and 'co-operation', referring to the relationships with specific (categories of) other actors. A non-eco strategy may be either confrontational or co-operative or perhaps both. An individual or organization may apply different strategies for different activities and in relation to different other actors as will be exemplified below. In this sense, the categories in Table 7.3 are not mutually exclusive.

This classification scheme will now be applied to some business organizations, CeOs and universities. It can be noted, however, that the scheme is also applicable to other organizational entities, such as trade organizations, labour unions and governmental agencies. By way of an example, for a long time the Swedish Environmental Protection Board (Naturvårdsverket) regarded environmental organizations (for instance The Environment Centre, to be discussed below) as its main enemies. In relation to these organizations the Swedish environmental administration tended to follow a strategy that can be described as belonging to the intermediate–confrontation category of Table 7.3. Administrators and environmentalists had different ideas about what to do for the environment.

Business Roles and Strategies for Ecological Sustainability

In the community of business organizations, one can probably find examples that relate to all six categories of strategies identified. There are still many defensive organizations. It is equally true that an increasing number of companies prepare for certification or are 'already' certified according to some system. These companies may belong to the intermediate or 'eco' category. Confrontation in relation to specific other actors is a possibility for each of the three main categories and the same can be said about co-operation.

In a recent PhD study presented at the University of Gothenburg, Birgitta Schwartz attempted to characterize the environmental strategies of three business corporations, Volvo, Tarkett and The Body Shop (Schwartz, 1997). During the period considered, Volvo worked largely through their public affairs department and attempted to co-operate with influential politicians and administrators in Stockholm. The previous head of Volvo has similarly been part of a Round Table for European Industrialists, one of its purposes being to influence EU transportation policies in Brussels towards building new motorways to link various industrial and other centres to each other.

Volvo can hardly be described as following an eco-strategy in all its activities. In terms of its core activities (the production of motor vehicles), I would rather place the company in the intermediate and 'window-dressing' category with an emphasis on co-operation with politicians and the national government (category d in Table 7.3). The purpose of most of its activities has been to pave the way for a continued increase in vehicle production and use. The idea is, it seems, to ensure that as little as possible happens to restrict private motoring and other forms of road traffic. In institutional advertising, Volvo presented itself as a responsible corporation in environmental terms, yet the company typically adopted a confrontational strategy (category c in Table 7.3) when negotiating with environmental organizations – such as the Environmental Centre (Miljöcentrum) Uppsala – over pollution abatement measures at their production facilities. In other areas of its activities, Volvo has come closer to adopting an eco-strategy, for instance by instituting an environmental award for scientists who contribute to an improved environment.

In her study, Schwartz came to the conclusion that Volvo used its power to influence the arena or scene, rather than to change its own strategy and action in terms of products and technology. Volvo could of course have also chosen a confrontational strategy in relation to the national government, for instance by threatening to move production to some other country. The 'outsourcing' phenomenon is, however, as I see it, as much a threat to business itself and, therefore, market capitalism and some business leaders may be reluctant to use this option.

The two other companies mentioned came closer to having an ecological strategy. Tarkett, a floor materials manufacturer, had some environmental problems with some of their product-lines and initiated research and development projects with the aim of being able to sell products which are environmentally more friendly. The company was successful, at least in part, in this strategic move. In this way, some areas of their activities remained in the non-eco category while another area moved to the eco category. Some confrontational tendencies (category e) were reported in relation to competing floor manufacturers, who argued that Tarkett was too sensitive to environmental interests.

As is well known, the third company, The Body Shop, has chosen an ecological strategy more systematically (categories e and f). As one example, this company has engaged in co-operative activities with Greenpeace.

Environmental Organizations' Roles and Strategies for Ecological Sustainability

I have chosen to refer to CeO rather than use the more common NGO terminology, because business organizations (most of them, anyway) are equally 'non-governmental'. (Today one even finds 'business environmental organizations', such as the WBCSD referred to earlier.) Environmental organizations by way of definition choose an environmental or ecological strategy (cf categories e and f in Table 7.3). Some of them, such as Greenpeace and the aforementioned Environmental Centre, are confrontational rather than co-operative in relation to other actor categories. They are seen as organizations with an independent voice who monitor both private and public sectors. Historically, environmental organizations, and their expertise, have played an important role in sharpening public awareness of and knowledge about environmental problems among establishment actors and citizens. As an example, Samuel Epstein identified a number of cases where specific chemicals were classified as cancerous by the relevant authorities in the USA and which consequently became the subject of prohibitions or other government measures (Epstein, 1978). He then tried to identify the actor categories that had initiated the debate and the legal processes that led to government action and found a number of so-called public interest organizations – Natural Resources Defense Council (NRDC), Environmental Defense Fund (EDF), Citizens for a Better Environment, Health Research Group of Public Citizens, Inc, Center for Science in the Public Interest, etc. Epstein also observed that university scholars, for instance those engaged in cancer research, had been remarkably passive on this subject.

The organizations mentioned claim to maintain their independence, but this does not exclude co-operative behaviour in some situations. As an example, Björn Gillberg, head of Miljöcentrum, has carried out an environmental investigation of the production facilities of H P Flügger, a firm in the paint industry, in preparation for certification according to ISO 14001 and EMAS. This activity was undertaken with the condition that any findings about environmental problems should be presented to the leadership of the company and representatives of the local and county environmental protection administration. Identified environmental problems, which are deemed to be serious by Gillberg and which are not dealt with in terms of practical measures by the company, could be reported to the media. Partly as a result of its strengthened environmental profile, H P Flügger has increased its market share in Sweden from 5 per cent to 15 per cent in three years. A 'knock-on' effect on other companies in the paint industry can also be observed.

While the Environment Centre has over the years worked mainly according to strategy e (eco-confrontational), a co-operative strategy (f, eco-co-operative) in relation to selected companies with a strong environmental leadership (eco-co-operative) is gaining ground. In my interview with Gillberg (4 January 1998), he made it clear that he co-operates only with one company in each trade or product area and that he sees it as more or less meaningless to co-operate with companies that belong to the 'window-dressing' category for environmental issues. Not only medium-sized companies, which can be expected to be more flexible, but also some large corporations like Scancem (previous Eurock) are involved in this kind of co-operation. Many years of dispute between Scancem and the Environment Centre were transformed to co-operation thanks to competent and strong leadership. Gillberg maintains that most large Swedish firms still lack this competent leadership in relation to environmental matters. The philosophy behind Björn Gillberg's work is discussed in a recent PhD thesis by Minna Gillberg (1999).

At the same time, there is a 'democratic' strategy connected with many environmental organizations in the sense that they often prefer to work through the media rather than co-operate directly with relevant state agencies or industries. It is believed that the role of 'educating' citizens and establishment actors is essential and that important problems should be discussed by as many people as possible, rather than be left to experts, some of whom have a very limited and specialized view of the world.

Finally, I would like to mention the Natural Step as a relatively new organization in Sweden, and one which has a strategy that differs somewhat from other environmental organizations. Their strategy is based on four ethical principles which advocate among other things, the avoidance of materials and chemicals that are toxic and biologically non-degradable. On the basis of this, their strategy can be described as one of dialogue with establishment actors and co-operation rather than confrontation (f, ie 'eco-co-operative'). Their focus is on positive examples that can be followed by others and there is an emphasis on professional networks such as 'engineers for the environment' and 'physicians for the environment'.

The Universities' Roles and Strategies for Ecological Sustainability

Universities are independent, at least in principle, and could therefore become important actors in relation to environmental issues. Traditional ideas about 'value neutrality' have too often led to a defensive or passive role in relation to the more important environmental issues. Cases of opportunistic behaviour in relation to perceived establishment interests are not difficult to find. On the other hand, one can identify scholars and teachers who have contributed constructively to an increased awareness and knowledge of environmental issues and who have been ready to criticize activities and production facilities, even in situations where this has been risky for their professional careers.

A broader understanding of epistemological issues (cf Table 2.1) is now gaining ground at many universities. It is no longer as controversial as it once was to take a stand on environmental issues. Some universities have chosen to openly present an environmental policy and have started to work towards becoming certified as part of ISO 14001. The university where I am employed, Mälardalen University, became certified under ISO 14001 in April 1999, and is the first university in Sweden, perhaps in Europe to do so – largely thanks to the work of the environmental co-ordinator Kristina von Oelreich. The environmental strategy of the university can be classified as being somewhere between the 'intermediate co-operative' and 'eco-co-operative' categories. Certification is of course only a beginning.

Universities in Sweden are expected to be active in three different but interrelated areas, namely education, research and interaction with outside actors as part of a co-operative learning process. Environmental criteria can be applied to projects and programmes in all three areas. The ecological economics programme for education and research at Mälardalen University is just one of many examples of what (hopefully) is going on at various educational levels and places around the globe.

Chapter 8

Epilogue

It has been argued throughout this book that economics is science in some sense, but that it is also ideology. Gunnar Myrdal is among those who have tried to remind his economist colleagues of the impossibility of a value-neutral economics – or any other social science. 'Values are always with us'. There is no view except from a particular viewpoint and whatever the viewpoint chosen, certain values are implied. This ideological aspect of economics is seldom taken seriously by economists. Many of them are apparently too concerned with their expert positions to openly declare or discuss their ideological viewpoints.

This tendency to avoid an open discussion about values has had the effect, desired by some, that economics is seen as a science not very different from physics or chemistry. An award in economics in memory of Alfred Nobel has been instituted by the Bank of Sweden. Although Gunnar Myrdal was awarded this prize in 1974 and a few other broad-minded economists have won it, such as Herbert Simon, Douglas North and Amartya Sen, the intended and actual impact of this award seems to be to further strengthen the position of neo-classical economics. Departments of economics at various Western and 'westernized' universities have been narrowed down to neo-classical economics. Interdisciplinary thinking seems to be limited to statistics and mathematics. A typical neo-classical economist does not understand the value either of alternative theoretical approaches within economics, or of theories emanating from other social sciences. Political science, as an example, is respected only to the extent that political scientists accept Public Choice theory and other neo-classical contributions.

At a recent seminar arranged as part of a research project, I had the opportunity to ask one of the leading neo-classical economists in Sweden, Mats Persson, whether he considered it a problem that economics departments in Sweden are now limited in their competence to neo-classical economics. Much research activity takes place these days under different labels, such as institutional economics, socio-economics, ecological economics, feministic economics and indeed in other social sciences, for instance business management and organization theory. I am glad to report that Persson responded that he saw the 'narrowness' in paradigmatic terms at departments of economics as a problem.

This judgement by Mats Persson can be taken as a positive sign, but on the whole little is done to improve the transdisciplinary competence of neo-classical economists. As other neo-classical economists, neo-classical environmental economists claim value neutrality and show hostility in relation to economists who suggest that non-neo-classical theoretical perspectives and paradigms can be very useful. In terms of our previous conceptual framework, their strategy is defensive and based on confrontation in relation to institutional economists like myself. Capacity building in this interdisciplinary direction would increase flexibility in a world undergoing rapid change. Conversely, a narrow competence is encumbered with considerable risk-taking and one can already observe in many places how economics departments are losing ground in terms of student enrolment to business management and the other social sciences.

The presence of values and ideology in teaching and research suggests that only a pluralistic attitude is compatible with democracy. As I see it, the neo-classical monopoly has to be abandoned. Unfortunately, little can be expected in terms of pluralism from departments of economics as they stand at the end of the 20th century. Neo-classical economists represent a relatively small and highly homogenous interest group which can be successful in rent-seeking terms even in the future. Neo-classical public choice theory is at least helpful in understanding the behaviour of neo-classical economists.

In order to strengthen democracy and open the doors for pluralism in economics, one has to rely mainly on platforms other than economics departments. I have myself moved back and forth between economics and business management departments over the years and have come to the conclusion that a department dominated by business economists and organization theorists is a much better place for new thinking in economics and on an interdisciplinary level. Such a readiness to cross borders between disciplines should be encouraged among old and young scholars alike.

In this book I have tried to articulate an alternative to the neo-classical view, beginning with the PEP, the PEO and a highly disaggregated idea about economics and efficiency. As a complement to traditional theories, an actor–network approach to markets and social change has been offered and PA proposed as an approach to decision-making. Together these components form a relatively coherent alternative microeconomics which adds, I believe, to our ability to understand and deal with problems of environment and development. Whereas neo-classical economics is connected with more extreme forms of market liberalism, our theory tends to be compatible with ecologism and socially and environmentally responsible forms of liberalism.

How Can All This be Applied?

What is the use of all this talk of pluralism, democracy, the PEP and ideological orientation? Can this conceptual frame of reference be used for practical purposes? Why not go directly to practical measures, for instance environmental charges or taxes? We already know that such instruments can be efficient. Is the frame of reference at all useful for research purposes?

I will try to respond to these questions.

Paradigms and Pluralism

I am sure that there is some possibility on the basis of present values and world views, of acting more directly through environmental laws, tax schemes and so on. But it should be recognized that there are limits to what one can accomplish within the scope of currently dominant world views, paradigms and ideologies. So, the fact that something can be done today in terms of practical measures does not make a dialogue about paradigms and ideologies less important. If one wants to change society in the direction of ecological sustainability, one cannot avoid the two related issues of paradigms in economics and ideologies in politics. The best one can do is to work on several levels. If extreme forms of market ideology (largely legitimized by neo-classical economics) is not challenged, then little will happen in terms of new environmental charges, taxes or more stringent legislation to change the behaviour of those individuals and organizations who systematically cause environmental damage.

Contrary to what many believe, articulation of – and debate about – paradigms and ideologies may be the quickest way to move forward toward a sustainable society. Many of those who are in favour of the status quo resist to the extreme this kind of debate about fundamental issues. Fortunately, the necessity of raising paradigm issues in relation to environment and development has been recognized, even in some establishment circles. As an example, the first conference with the International Society for Ecological Economics took place on the premises of the World Bank. At the time Robert Goodland and Herman Daly were employed by the Bank and both were known for their scepticism in relation to the monopoly of neo-classical economics (Goodland and Ledec, 1987; Daly and Cobb, 1989). Another scholar who participated at that conference, Michael Colby, had previously written a World Bank paper, where he drew distinctions between five theoretical perspectives concerning the management of natural resources, from 'frontier economics' to 'deep ecology' (Colby, 1990).

Similar attempts to increase consciousness about paradigms in economics can now be found in publications by Swedish authorities. In 1994, the 'Eco-Cycle Commission' arranged a seminar to discuss product policy in industry with participants from the USA, Canada and some European countries, known for their endeavours to do something about the environmental crisis (for instance Germany, The Netherlands, and other Scandinavian countries). Several participants pointed to the need to discuss world views and paradigms (Ministry of Environment, 1995). As far as I can judge, no neo-classical environmental economist participated in that seminar.

Similarly, research in economics has to become interdisciplinary and pluralistic. Philosophers can study the kind of ethics emphasized in economics (utilitarianism of a specific kind) and discuss the possibilities for alternative ethical approaches (deontological, etc) in economics. This is being done in a comprehensive project co-ordinated by Carl-Henrik Grenholm, Professor of Ethics at the Department of Theology, Uppsala University. Advisors and PhD students from three different departments (ethics, philosophy and business administration) are involved (Grenholm and Helgesson, 1998). One of the PhD students, Ann-Cathrin Jarl, takes as her starting point feministic economics for a study of social issues in developing countries. Feministic economics can be seen as an ideological criticism (although it is not always presented as such) of neo-classical economics. In a special issue of *Ecological Economics* edited by Ellie Perkins (1997), a number of contributions were presented as examples of 'feministic economics'. There is an ambition to go 'beyond Economic Man' and make things that matter for women (like 'unpaid work') visible in economic analyses.

The imperative of pluralism has the effect of increasing consciousness about paradigms and ideologies. Each student normally prefers and believes in a specific paradigm and should demonstrate why this particular paradigm has been chosen and preferably make some comparisons with alternatives that have been rejected as less relevant or useful. Pluralism does not normally mean that the student has to apply different paradigms in the same study. But the social and institutional context and power situation at economics departments may be such that it is not possible to exclude the neo-classical approach by option. I was recently involved in the evaluation process of a PhD study on how Norwegian farmers use fertilizers. It is an unusually ambitious study where neo-classical as well as institutional approaches are presented and applied in field studies. So, proposals in the direction of 'methodological pluralism' or 'paradigmatic pluralism' can also be taken literally which represents an added value (Vedeld, 1994, 1998).

In addition two recent Finnish studies are relevant to the present discussion. Anja Kiviluoto identifies four versions of institutionalism: 'mainstream institutionalism', the 'Wisconsin school', a 'co-evolutionary tradition' and 'William Kapp's institutional ideas', and relates them to environmental and development issues. She comes out in favour of the latter European tradition, which also includes Gunnar Myrdal and a Finnish group at Helsinki University, for instance Kauko Hahtola, Markku Turtiainen, Antti Leskinen (Kiviluoto, 1997). Minna Halme has written a PhD thesis in Business Administration on how world views and paradigms change when environmental values are internalized by actors in business, more precisely two Finnish paper companies (Halme, 1997).

In the field of 'business and environment', Richard Welford (1996) has focused on EMSs as well as arguing in favour of more critical research by business economists in relation to current trends with the emergence of organizations such as the WBCSD. It appears that 'the Greening of Business' in the years to come can be a very fruitful area for creative work and for new thinking in economics and business administration (Welford, 1997a, 1997b).

Studies on Actors, Relationships and Institutions

Environmental problems become visible in soil, water and air. Groundwater can be polluted, biological diversity may be reduced. But it is increasingly understood that environmental problems are also visible in some sense in the values, thinking patterns and life-styles of various actors. This is one aspect of the total complex problem. Studies on how actors feel, think, argue and relate to each other and behave are therefore extremely important. Examples of such studies have been given, for instance the two Finnish studies mentioned above and the report by Lönngren and Axelsson on a 'responsibility trap' discussed in Chapter 7.

One example of a challenge for future studies is to describe and evaluate the life-styles of individuals in relation to environmental problems. Attempts can also be made to characterize the environmental strategies of specific actors in relation to other actors or actor categories (cf Table 7.3).

Organizational and institutional change within business and other organizations (for instance the implementation of ISO 14001 or EMAS) is another area of interest. The same is true of institutional change at the level of trade organizations, nations or even internationally.

Decision-Making, Evaluation and Conflict Management

A third area for environmental and development studies can be described by the following three points:

1   descriptive studies on policy and decision-making processes;
2   ex-post evaluations of activities, investment decisions and policies;
3   approaches to decision-making, for instance investment decisions in business or at a societal level.

Economists generally emphasize decisions related to the future, for instance investment decisions and what they refer to as efficient resource allocation. Our approach suggests that descriptive studies of policy formation and decision-making processes are also of interest (cf 1, above). How does democracy function in practice? Which are the actors and how do they perceive their roles? How does expert judgement enter the process? What kinds of study are carried out and by whom? What were the main moral conflicts and sources of disagreement (cf Gutman and Thompson, 1996) and how were they handled as part of the policy formation or decision process?

Examples of follow-up studies (by Hillring and Forsberg) were given in Chapter 6 (cf 2 above). Learning from the past is a way of preparing for the future. Hillring took as his starting point a set of decisions made by a public agency in the past for environmental and other reasons to support specific activities or projects by private companies. He then followed up the results or impacts. How do these impacts compare with the intentions expressed in written form by those who once applied for financial support?

Retrospective studies could also be broader in scope. In a recent study, Pascal Delisle focuses on the development history of the Amazonian parts of Colombia and discusses the prospects for sustainable development in the same area (Delisle, 1998). His approach is multidimensional and multidisciplinary and he refers to a holistic conception of economics where monetary and non-monetary impacts are kept separate. The philosophy of PA is preferred when compared with conventional economic analysis as being more in line with the complexity of the problems faced in this particular part of the world.

The third point above refers to the more traditional area of future oriented decisions. A number of studies using PA have been carried out by students in Sweden, Finland and Norway at various levels including at PhD level (for an overview see Brorsson, 1995). Jan-Erik Mattsson's (1991) study of alternative future energy systems in the municipality of Hedemora is one example and Kjell-Åke Brorsson's study of the regulation of a lake's water level in the county of Småland is another. Rather than limiting attention to variables normally considered by economists, Brorsson made an interdisciplinary study and consulted a number of experts, in fields as diverse as hydrology and wildlife biology (Brorsson, 1995).

In a study at the Agricultural University of Norway, Mafunda and Navrud (1995) compared various ideological alternatives for the future development of a river basin in Tanzania. Finally, Antti Leskinen wrote a PhD thesis in which positional analysis was applied to road planning. Rather than seeing his study as exclusively a technical process, Leskinen emphasized how various affected parties and other actors could participate in a problem solving process, partly carried out separately from the usual planning process in the road planning administration (Leskinen, 1994).

THE ROLE OF UNIVERSITIES

It is easy to criticize industry, politicians, farmers and many others for the sad state of the human environment and such critical evaluation should continue and is partly the responsibility of universities. I believe, contrary to many others, that confrontation is sometimes needed although co-operation and voluntary agreements of various kinds should be the main strategy.

While we as actors within universities can use our relatively independent role and participate in public debate, we should also take a look at our own organizations from an environmental point of view. EMSs are as relevant for universities as for other organizations and environmental criteria can be applied in the evaluation of educational and research programmes. Much remains to be done at most universities and other schools in these respects. Education as well as research and development are critical activities in a transformation to a sustainable society.

There are special reasons to introduce some new thinking into the disciplines of economics and business management. Issues of values, ideologies and paradigms have to be discussed much more openly and the only reasonable way to proceed in a democracy is to accept some degree of pluralism in the sense that the theoretical perspectives presented reflect a large part of the spectrum of values in a particular society. The neo-classical tradition of pointing out 'scientific solutions to political problems' has to be broken. A more humble attitude of illuminating an issue will re-establish confidence in economics and other disciplines.

Not only is there a political and ideological element in research and education, but perhaps there is also a personal element. Our reference to PEP can be interpreted in these terms. The scholar tries to write something which is relevant and useful for many individuals, but also her or his personality is reflected in the final product. Such statements take us further away from the traditions of objectivity and general laws and closer to the newer fields of hermeneutics and phenomenology. I participated recently in an interdisciplinary workshop on environmental policy in Pori, Finland arranged by Yrjö Haila. The workshop took place in an art museum and for the three days no less than three art exhibitions were visited by the workshop participants. There may have been a hidden message from the organizers in this, in the sense that science and art are perhaps not as different as commonly understood. No one doubts the presence of personality in art, but what about science? An attempt to consciously recognize how our personalities affect what we are writing is perhaps another way – in addition to the ideological element – of reaching a better understanding of each other.

References

Ackerman, Frank (1997) 'Consumed in theory: Alternative perspectives on the economics of consumption', *Journal of Economic Issues*, 31(3), pp651–64

Alchian, Armen A (1950) 'Uncertainty, evolution, and economic theory', *Journal of Political Economy*, June, pp211–21

Alsmark, Gunnar (ed) (1997) *Skjorta eller själ? Kulturella identiteter i tid och rum* (Shirt or soul? Cultural identities in time and space), Studentlitteratur, Lund

Becker, Henk (1997) *Social Impact Assessment*, UCL Press, London

Biesecker, Adelheid, Wolfram Elsner and Klaus Grenzdörffer (eds) (1998) *Ökonomie der Betroffenen und Mitwirkenden: Erweiterte Stakeholder Prozesse*, Centaurus-Verlagsgesellschaft, Pfaffenweiler

Brorsson, Kjell-Åke (1995) *Metodutveckling av positionsanalysen genom tillämpning på Assjö kvarn. Hållbar utveckling i relation till miljö och sårbarhet* (Methodological development of positional analysis. An application to Assjö water mill), Swedish University of Agricultural Sciences, Department of Economics, Dissertations 14, Uppsala

Colby, Michael E (1990) *Environmental Management in Development*, World Bank Discussion Paper 80, The World Bank, Washington, DC

Cornland, Deborah (1997) Stockholm Environment Institute, 6 November, personal communication

Costanza, Robert (1989) 'What is ecological economics?' *Ecological Economics*, 1(1), pp1–7

Costanza, Robert (ed) (1991) *Ecological Economics. The science and management of sustainability*, Columbia University Press, New York

Costanza, Robert, John Cumberland, Herman Daly, Robert Goodland and Richard Norgaard (1997) *An Introduction to Ecological Economics*, St Lucie Press, Boca Raton FL

Czarniawska, Barbara (1997) *Narrating the Organization. Dramas in Institutional Identity*, University of Chicago Press, Chicago

Daly, Herman E and John R Cobb Jr (1989) *For the Common Good. Redirecting the economy toward community, the environment and a sustainable future*, Beacon Press, Boston

Delisle, Pascal (1998) *Colonisation agricole et developpement soutenable en fôret tropicale: pour une approche multidimensionelle. Le cas d'Amazonie Colombienne.* PhD thesis, Economic Sciences, University of Paris I, Pantheon-Sorbonne

Dobson, Andrew (1995) *Green Political Thought* (second edition), Routledge, London

Eccleshall, Robert (1994) 'Liberalism'. In: Eccleshall et al, 1994, pp28–59

Eccleshall, Robert, Vincent Geoghegan, Richard Jay, Michael Kenny, Iain MacKenzie and Rick Wilford (1994) *Political Ideologies. An introduction* (second edition), Routledge, London

Ehrenfeld, John (1995) 'Industrial ecology: A strategic framework for product policy and other sustainable practices'. In: *Green Goods*, Ministry of Environment, Ecocycle Commission, Report 1995:5, pp34–67

Epstein, Samuel S (1978) *The Politics of Cancer*, Sierra Club, San Francisco

Etzioni, Amitai (1988) *The Moral Dimension: Toward a new economics*, Free Press, New York

Etzioni, Amitai (1992) 'The I & We Paradigm'. In: Ekins, Paul and Manfred Max-Neef (eds) *Real-Life Economics: Understanding wealth creation*, pp48–53, Routledge, London

Faucheux, Sylvie, Martin O'Connor and Jan van der Straaten (1998) *Sustainable Development: Concepts, Rationalities and Strategies*, Kluwer, Dortrecht

Fischer, Frank (1990) *Technocracy and the Politics of Expertise*, Sage, Newbury Park

Ford, David (ed) (1990) *Understanding Business Markets. Interaction, Relationships, Networks*, Academic Press, London

Forsberg, Göran (1993) *Finns ekologiskt hållbara energisystem? En uppföljning och konsekvensbeskrivning för Kils kommun* (Energy systems and ecological sustainability. The municipality of Kil as a case), Swedish University of Agricultural Sciences, Department of Economics, Report 63, Uppsala

Fukuyama, Francis (1989) 'The end of history?' *National Interest*, Summer, pp3–18

Fukuyama, Francis (1992) *The End of History and the Last Man*, Free Press, New York

Fusfeld, Daniel R (1994) *The Age of the Economist* (seventh edition), Harper Collins, New York

Gilbert, M J (1993) *Achieving Environmental Management Standards: a step by step guide to meeting BS 7750*, The Institute of Management, Pitman Publishing, London

Gillberg, Björn (1998) Environmental Centre, Uppsala, 4 January, personal communication

Gillberg, Minna (1999) *From Green Image to Green Practise. Normative action and self-regulation*, Lund University, Department of Sociology, Lund Studies in Sociology of Law, 6, Lund

Goodland, Robert and Georg Ledec (1987) 'Neoclassical economics and principles of sustainable development', *Ecological Modelling*, 38(1/2), pp29–46

Goodwin, Neva, Frank Ackerman and David Kiron (eds) (1997) *The Consumer Society*, Island Press, Washington, DC

Grenholm, Carl-Henrik and Gert Helgesson (1998) *Ethics, Economics and Feminism*, Department of Theology, Uppsala University, Studies in ethics and economics, 3, Uppsala

Gutman, Amy and Dennis Thompson (1996) *Democracy and Disagreement. Why moral conflict cannot be avoided in politics, and what should be done about it*, Belknap Press, Cambridge, Mass

Håkansson, Håkan and Ivan Snehota (eds) (1995) *Developing Relationships in Business Networks*, Routledge, London

Halme, Minna (1997) *Environmental Management Paradigm Shifts in Business Enterprises. Organizational learning relating to recycling and forest management issues in two Finnish paper companies*, Academic Dissertation, University of Tampere, School of Business Administration, Tampere

Hannigan, John A (1995) *Environmental Sociology. A social constructionist perspective*, Routledge, London

Henderson, Hazel (1981) *The Politics of the Solar Age: Alternatives to economics*, Anchor Press, New York

Hillring, Bengt (1996) *Forest Fuel Systems Utilising Tree Sections. System evaluation and development of evaluation methodology*, Swedish University of Agricultural Sciences, Faculty of Forestry, Studia Forestalia Suecica, No 200, Uppsala

Hirschman, Albert O (1970) *Exit, Voice, and Loyalty*, Harvard University Press, Cambridge, Mass

Hodgson, Geoffrey M, Warren J Samuels and Mark R Tool (eds) (1994) *The Elgar Companion to Institutional and Evolutionary Economics*, Edward Elgar, Cheltenham

Howard, John A (1963) *Marketing Management. Analysis and Planning*, Irwing, Homewood, Ill

Jansson, Ann-Mari (ed) (1984) *Integration of Economy and Ecology. An outlook for the eighties* (Proceedings from the Wallenberg Symposia), Askö Laboratory, Stockholm University, Stockholm

Kapp K William (1970, first edition 1950) *The Social Costs of Private Enterprise*, Shocken Books, New York

Kenny, Michael (1994) 'Ecologism'. In: Eccleshall et al, 1994, pp218–51

Kiviluoto, Anja (1997) *Peter Söderbaum's Position in the Field of Institutional Economics*, (Masters' thesis). University of Helsinki, Department of Economics and Management, Environmental Economics, Helsinki. (Reproduced as 'Institutional Economists in Relation to Environmental Issues' in Department of Business Studies and Informatics, Report 1, 1999, Mälardalen University, Västerås)

Kohler Riessman, Catherine (1993) *Narrative Analysis*, Sage, London

Köhn, Jörg, John Gowdy, Friedrich Hinterberger and Jan van der Straaten (1999) *Sustainability in Question. The search for a new conceptual framework*, Edward Elgar, Cheltenham

Korten, David C (1995) *When Corporations Rule the World*, Kumarian Press, West Hartford

Kotler, Philip (1997) *Marketing Management* (9th edition), Prentice Hall, Englewood Cliffs

Krishnan, Rajaram, Jonathan M Harris and Neva R Goodwin (eds) (1995) *A Survey of Ecological Economics* (Frontier Issues in Economic Thought), Island Press, Washington, DC

Kuhn, Thomas S (1970) *The Structure of Scientific Revolutions* (second edition), University of Chicago Press, Chicago

Larsson, Reidar (1997) *Politiska ideologier i vår tid* (Political ideologies of our time), Studentlitteratur, Lund

Leipert, Christian and Rolf Steppacher (eds) (1987) *K William Kapp. Für eine ökosociale Ökonomie. Entwürfe und Ideen – Ausgewählte Aufsätze*, Fischer Verlag, Frankfurt am Main

Leskinen, Antti (1994) *Environmental Planning as Learning: The Principles of Negotiation, Disaggregative Decision Making and Parallel Organization in Developing the Road Administration* (PhD Thesis), University of Helsinki, Department of Economics and Management. Publications No 5, Environmental Economics, Helsinki

Lönngren, Mats and Svante Axelsson (1995) *Hinder och möjligheter för miljöarbete – en kartläggning av centrala aktörers problembilder* (Barriers and opportunities for environmental work. Mapping the problem images of influential actors), Swedish University of Agricultural Sciences, Department of Extension, Report 3, Uppsala

Mafunda, Dugushilu and Ståle Navrud (1995) 'Positional analysis applied to water pollution problems in developing countries'. In: Dinar, Ariel and Edna Tusak Loehman (eds) *Water Quantity/Quality Management and Conflict Resolution. Institutions, Processes, and Economic Analyses*, Praeger, London

Magnusson, Lars and Jan Ottosson (eds) (1997) *Evolutionary Economics and Path Dependence*, Edward Elgar, Cheltenham

March, James G (1994) *A Primer in Decision Making*, Free Press, New York

Mattsson, Jan-Erik (1991) *Val av energisystem för fjärrvärmeverk i Hedemora – försök till allsidig belysning* (Selection of system for the district heating plant in Hedemora – a many-sided illumination), Swedish University of Agricultural Sciences, Faculty of Forestry, Department of Operational Efficiency, Report no 190, Garpenberg

McCloskey, D N (1983) 'The rhetoric of economics', *Journal of Economic Literature*, 21, pp481–517

Ministry of Environment, Eco-Cycle Commission (1995) *Green Goods*, Stockholm

Ministry of Environment (1997) Statens offentliga utredningar 1997:84. *En hållbar kemikaliepolitik* (Environmental policy for chemicals), Betänkande av kemikommittén, Stockholm

Ministry of Environment (1997) *Agenda 21 in Sweden, National Report. From Environmental Protection to Sustainable Development*, Stockholm

Mishan, Ezra J (1980) 'How valid are economic evaluations of allocative changes?' *Journal of Economic Issues*, 14 (March), pp143–61

Morgan, Gareth (1986) *Images of Organization*, Sage, London

Mueller D C (1979) *Public Choice*, Cambridge University Press, Cambridge

Myrdal, Gunnar (1975, first edition 1972) *Against the Stream. Critical essays on economics*, Random House, New York

Myrdal, Gunnar (1978) 'Institutional economics' *Journal of Economic Issues*, 12(4), (December), pp771–83

Netherwood, Alan (1996) 'Environmental management systems'. In: Welford, Richard *Corporate Environmental Management. Systems and strategies*, pp35–58, Earthscan, London

Norgaard, Richard B (1994) *Development Betrayed. The end of progress and a coevolutionary revisioning of the future*, Routledge, London

North, Douglass C (1990) *Institutions, Institutional Change and Economic Performance*, Cambridge University Press, Cambridge

NUTEK (1993) Department of Energy Efficiency, *Purchasers' Requirements Dictate Development: A Study of Technology Procurement*, Stockholm

O'Connor, Martin and Clive Spash (1999) *Valuation and the Environment. Theory, method and practice*, Edward Elgar, Cheltenham

Olson, Mancur (1982) *The Rise and Decline of Nations. Economic growth, stagflation and social rigidities*, Yale University Press, New Haven, Conn

Passet, René (1997) 'ESEE what for?' *ESEE Newsletter* No 1 (March)

Pearce, David W, Anil Markandya and Edward B Barbier (1989) *Blueprint for a Green Economy*, Earthscan, London

Pearce, David W and R Kerry Turner (1990) *Economics of Natural Resources and the Environment*, Harvester Wheatsheaf, New York

Perkins, Ellie (ed) (1997) 'Women, ecology and economics' (Special Issue), *Ecological Economics*, 20, pp105–85

Ramstad, Yngve (1987) 'Free Trade Versus Fair Trade: Import barriers as a problem of reasonable value', *Journal of Economic Issues*, 21(1), pp5–32

Randall, Alan (1986), 'Institutional and neoclassical approaches to environmental policy'. In: Tim T Phipps, Pierre R Crosson and Kenneth A Price
(eds) *Agriculture and Environment*, pp205–24. The National Centre for
Food and Agricultural Policy. Annual Policy Review, 1986, Resources for
the Future, Washington, DC

Rossini, Frederick A and Alan L Porter (eds) (1983) *Integrated Impact
Assessment*, Social Impact Assessment Series, No 8, Westview Press,
Boulder

Rutherford, Malcolm (1994) 'Commons John R'. In: Hodgson, Geoffrey M
et al (eds) *The Elgar Companion to Institutional and Evolutionary
Economics*, Edward Elgar, Cheltenham

Sachs, Ignacy (1976) 'Environment and styles of development'. In:
Matthews, William H (ed) *Outer Limits and Human Needs*, pp41–65,
Dag Hammarskjöld Foundation, Uppsala

Sachs, Ignacy (1984) 'Strategies of eco-development', *Ceres. FAO Review on
Agriculture and Development*, 17(4), pp17–21

Sagoff, Mark (1988) *The Economy of the Earth. Philosophy, law and the
environment*, Cambridge University Press, Cambridge

Samuels, Warren (1995) 'The present state of institutional economics'
Cambridge Journal of Economics 19, pp569–90

Schumacher, Friedrich (1973) *Small is Beautiful. Economics as if people
mattered*, Harper & Row, London

Schwartz, Birgitta (1997) *Det miljöanpassade företaget – strategiska uppträ-
danden på den institutionella scenen* (Adaptation of business to
environment – strategic behaviour on the institutional scene), Nerenius
and Santérus, Stockholm

Self, Peter (1975) *Econocrats and the Policy Process. The politics and philosophy of Cost–Benefit Analysis*, Macmillan, London

Sen, Amartya (1987) *On Ethics and Economics*, Basil Blackwell, New York

Simmons, Peter and Brian Wynne (1993) 'Responsible Care: "Trust, credibil-
ity, and environmental management"'. In: Fischer, Kurt and Johan Schot
(eds) *Environmental Strategies for Industry. International perspectives,
research needs and policy implications*, Island Press, Washington, DC

Simon, Herbert (1945) *Administrative Behaviour*, Free Press, New York

Simon, Herbert (1983) *Reason in Human Affairs*, Basil Blackwell, London

Söderbaum, Peter (1973) *Positionsanalys vid beslutsfattande of planering.
Ekonomisk analys på tvärvetenskaplig grund* (Positional Analysis for
Decision Making and Planning. Economic analysis on an interdisciplinary
basis), Esselte Studium, Stockholm

Söderbaum, Peter (1980) 'Towards a reconciliation of economics and
ecology', *European Review of Agricultural Economics*, 7, 1, pp55–77

Söderbaum, Peter (1982) 'Ecological imperatives for public policy', *Ceres.
FAO Review for Agriculture and Development* 15, 2, pp28–30

Söderbaum, Peter (1983) 'Ezra Mishan on economic evaluation. A comment', *Journal of Economic Issues* 17 (March), pp206–13

Söderbaum, Peter (1991) 'Environmental and agricultural issues: What is the alternative to Public Choice theory?' In: Partha Dasgupta (ed) *Issues in Contemporary Economics. Volume 3. Policy and Development*, pp24–42, Macmillan, London

Söderbaum, Peter (1992), 'Neoclassical and institutional approaches to development and the environment', *Ecological Economics*, 5, pp127–44

Söderbaum, Peter (1993) *Ekologisk ekonomi. Miljö och utveckling i ny belysning* (Ecological economics. New perspectives on environment and development), Studentlitteratur, Lund

Söderbaum, Peter (1999a) 'Values, ideology and politics in ecological economics', *Ecological Economics*, 28, pp161–70

Söderbaum, Peter (1999b) 'Political Economic Person and Political Economic Organization: A conceptual framework for business environmental policy', *The Journal of Interdisciplinary Economics*, 10, pp195–211

Tietenberg, Tom (1992) *Environmental and Natural Resource Economics* (third edition), HarperCollins, New York

Toulmin, Stephen (1990) *Cosmopolis. The Hidden Agenda of Modernity*, University of Chicago Press, Chicago

Ullman, John E and Roy Preiswerk (eds) (1985) *The Humanization of the Social Sciences. K William Kapp*, University Press of America, Lanham

Ulrich, Peter (1997) *Integrative Wirtschaftsethik. Grundlagen einer lebensdienlichen Ökonomie*, Verlag Paul Haupt, Bern

Vedeld, Pål O (1994) 'The environment and interdisciplinarity. Ecological and neoclassical economical approaches to the use of natural resources', *Ecological Economics* 10(1), pp1–13.

Vedeld, Pål O (1998) *Farmers and Fertilizers: A Study of Adaptation and Response to Price Change among Norwegian Farmers*, Doctor scientiarum thesis 1997:14, Agricultural University of Norway, Department of Economics and Social Sciences, Dissertation no 1998:3

Welford Richard (1996) *Corporate Environmental Management: Systems and Strategies*, Earthscan, London

Welford, Richard (1997a) *Corporate Environmental Management 2: Culture and Organizations*, Earthscan, London

Welford Richard (1997b) *Hijacking Environmentalism: Corporate Responses to Sustainable Development*, Earthscan, London

World Business Council for Sustainable Development (WBCSD) (1997) *Signals of Change. Business Progress Towards Sustainable Development*, Geneva

World Commission on Environment and Development (1987) *Our Common Future*, Oxford University Press, Oxford

Worldwatch Institute (1997) *State of the World 1997*, Earthscan, London

Von Wright, Georg Henrik (1986) *Vetenskapen och förnuftet. Ett försök till orientering* (Science and reason. An introduction), Bonniers, Stockholm

Index